THE
Reader's Digest
GOOD
BEACH
GUIDE

With Ordnance Survey Maps

MARINE CONSERVATION
SOCIETY

David & Charle

D0259125

A David & Charles Book
Copyright text © Marine Conservation Society, 1994
Maps reproduced from Ordnance Survey Landranger 1:50,000 series with the permission of Her
Majesty's Stationery Office © Crown Copyright, Permit No 680 – Northern Ireland
First published 1994

A catalogue record for this book is available from the British Library.

ISBN 0 7153 0258 2

Produced by The Cooling Brown Partnership, Hampton, Middlesex
Edited by Catherine Loretto
Printed by Butler & Tanner Ltd, Frome
for David & Charles
Brunel House, Newton Abbot, Devon

Acknowledgements
The information from which this guide has been compiled was supplied by the National Rivers
Authorities of England and Wales, the River Purification Boards of Scotland, the Department of the
Environment for Northern Ireland, the States of Jersey, Guernsey and the Isle of Man, the Isles of Scilly
Environmental Trust, the private water service companies, the Water and Sewerage sections of the
Regional Councils of Scotland, Environmental Health Offices and Tourism Offices of local authorities,
the National Trust, the National Trust for Scotland, and data from the Reader's Digest Beachwatch
survey which was co-ordinated by the Marine Conservation Society.

All information received up until 1 January 1994 has been included in this guide. The Marine
Conservation Society and David & Charles take no responsibility for changes occuring after
compilation of the work.

I would like to thank all those who responded to my questionnaires, Reader's Digest for sponsoring
the publication, all the staff, volunteers and Conservation Advisory Council of the Marine Conservation
Society for support and assistance during the collation of this guide, particularly Rob Keddie for
processing the data and Liz Lewis for tracking down the photographs, and finally thank you to my
friends and family for their support and encouragement.
Cait Loretto, Marine Conservation Society

Picture credits
P.1,9,217 MCS. P.6,25,26,31 Paul Watts. P.7,118,167 David Woodfall. P.8,63,68,117 Carolyn
Heeps/MCS. P.8,126 Sue Gubbay/MCS. P.9 Richard Caines/MCS. P.12,107 Bob Earll/MCS. P.13 Rees
Cox. P.14,18,34,43,50,57,65 Mike Williams/Countryside Commission. P.20 Bill Foster/MCS. P.28,173
Mark Boulton/ICCE. P.32 H.P.Moorland/ICCE. P.37,39 NT/Dan Flunder. P.46 South Devon Heritage
Coast Service. P.48,52,54 South Hams Tourism. P.60 David Garner/NT. P.67,156,174,180,183 Andrew
Davies. P.73 Bournemouth Tourism. P.75 Sarah Welton/MCS. P.77 RYA. P.78 IWTO/Peter Titmuss.
P.80,94 Dover District Council. P.82,85 Gosport Tourist Information. P.86 Havant Borough Council.
P.89 Chichester District Council. P.97 Thanet District Council. P.99 Canterbury Tourism. P.100,109
RSPB. P.101 Paul Glendell. P.103,105 Suffolk Coastal District Council. P.111 King's Lynn & West
Norfolk B.C. P.112 Sea Mammal Research Unit. P.121 Tony Hopkins/Countryside Commission. P.123
Countryside Commission. P.127 Cait Loretto/MCS. P.134,149 Roy Jarman/MCS. P.137 East Lothian
Tourist Board. P.139 Peter McCarron. P.141 St Andrews & N.E. Fife Tourist Board. P.143 Niall Benvie.
P.145 Gordon Henderson. P.147 Aberdeen Tourist Board. P.151 Sutherland Tourist Board. P.163,178
Wales Tourist board. P.165 Archway Publicity/Countryside Commission. P.168,170,176 Martin
Trelawney/Countryside Commission. P.185 Rose Winnall/ICCE. P.188 Mike Williams
P.191,193,195 Northern Island Tourist Board. P.199 Brian Green. P.196,200,203,205,207,209,211 Jersey
Tourism.

PREFACE

We use our coast for recreation, as a source of food and as a dustbin. Each day around one thousand million litres (three hundred million gallons) of raw or partially treated sewage is discharged into the seas around Britain. Sewage-related debris spoils beautiful beaches, sewage can damage marine life, and bathing in sewage-contaminated water can cause illness. This book will enable you, the reader, to make an informed choice about where to bathe. The guide features beaches which have good water quality and should not be affected by sewage. It also gives details of over five hundred beaches, many of which are badly affected by sewage. Britain has a beautiful coastline and we should treat it with the respect it deserves. If you care about the state of the beaches you visit and the quality of the seawater in which you and your family swim, read *The Reader's Digest Good Beach Guide* before you go.

FOREWORD

INFORMATION IS POWER. IF YOU'VE GOT IT, YOU CAN DO SOMETHING WITH IT. IF YOU HAVEN'T, YOU ARE DEAD IN THE WATER — METAPHORICALLY SPEAKING, OF COURSE!

•

And that is why I was delighted to be asked to write the foreword to *The Reader's Digest Good Beach Guide* produced by the Marine Conservation Society. It tells you everything you need to know about the quality of the bathing water off the UK's many and varied beaches, and in so doing, gives you the power to make personal choices far more wisely than you would otherwise be able to do. If enough people make those choices on the basis of sound, scientific information, then the quality of the whole environment can be slowly but surely improved.

In that context, tourism is a hugely important industry for the UK. And it is very competitive. We don't have to put up with poor quality; and we shouldn't be prepared to. And when it comes to seaside holidays, quality all depends on the weather (over which even Michael Fish has no control), the place where you are staying (which usually depends on financial circumstances), and the quality of the nearest beaches (where it is not money that counts, but what is actually in the water).

So what could be more irrational than going off to the seaside for a couple of weeks with the kids without the remotest inkling as to the quality of the water they'll soon be dunking themselves in?

Year by year, people are wising up to these things. Directors of tourism know that they are in trouble if their beach gets a lousy write-up and in clover if it is given the all-clear. Hoteliers depend in part on having clean safe beaches to which to direct people. A dirty beach is a drain on the local economy.

Courtesy of the European Union, the legislation is now in place progressively to improve water quality standards at our beaches. And they are steadily improving, after years of quite disgraceful neglect by the erstwhile water authorities.

But the pace of change is still very slow. By and large, the new water service companies are doing only the minimum necessary to comply with law rather than what is now technologically possible. And the Government itself is now backtracking on the pledge it has made on countless occasions to ensure compliance of that law by 1995.

So the balance of power in information cuts both ways. By using this guide, the Marine Conservation Society hopes that you have a happier, higher quality holiday. But to do their job properly, they need information from you – the good, the bad, and the all-too-often extremely ugly! And they need your continuing active support in pressuring local authorities, water companies and national politicians to help deliver to us the environment we and our children deserve.

Jonathon Porritt.

CONTENTS

CHAPTER ONE

INTRODUCTION

*Britain has highly diverse coastal scenery. This fascinating rock formation is at Millhook
Beach, near Widemouth Bay, North Cornwall.*

Nearly everyone who lives in Britain has visited the coast. Britain is, after all, an island
nation and we are never more than 200 km (120 miles) from the coast anywhere in
the British Isles. Our coast is around 15,000 km (9,000 miles) long and the coastal scenery
is highly diverse, ranging from dramatic granite cliffs to seemingly endless salt marshes.
We should treat the coast with the respect that it deserves, and make sure that we keep it
fit for wildlife and our own use.

We use our coast and coastal waters for many different purposes: recreation, as a source
of food and as a dustbin. The coast is under constant pressure. Each day over one
thousand million litres (three hundred million gallons) of raw or screened sewage (which
is effectively raw) is discharged into the sea. Sewage can damage marine life, cause illness
and reduce some of our finest stretches of coast to an aesthetically revolting mess. A recent

survey, conducted by the National Rivers Authority in the south-west of England, showed that out of 202 beaches only eight were judged to be free of sewage related debris; many beaches were found to be objectionable.

The quality of the beaches and bathing waters of Britain has been the subject of controversy and heated debate for the past four decades. The first 'Golden List of Beaches' giving details of beaches contaminated by sewage was produced by Tony and Daphne Wakefield following the death of their daughter from polio. They believed she contracted the disease whilst swimming in sewage contaminated water. The Wakefields established the Coastal Anti-Pollution League which merged with the Marine Conservation Society (MCS), an environmental organisation working exclusively to safeguard the marine environment, in the 1980s. The Marine Conservation Society have been calling for improvements in the treatment of our coast and coastal waters for many years, and have been particularly active in the field of sewage pollution. This guide is the seventh produced by the MCS and is a continuation and development from the very first 'Golden List of Beaches'.

The EC Blue Flag at Whitesands Bay, Pembrokeshire.

There is much confusion about the state of British Beaches and much conflicting information, including many different awards and accolades given to beaches. The major ones are the European Blue Flag and the Seaside Awards (a yellow and blue flag). These flags can be awarded to beaches with widely differing water quality. Beaches flying the European Blue Flag or the Premier Seaside Award should be meeting the Guideline Standards of the EC Bathing Water Directive and should therefore have acceptable water quality. However, the standard Seaside Awards can be allocated to areas with far lower water quality and certain beaches flying a Seaside Award flag may only be achieving the minimum standards required by law and will almost certainly be contaminated with sewage.

MCS would like to see an award flag, of any colour, indicating excellent water quality; until these flags are awarded to only those beaches with such water quality there will be continuing confusion about their meaning.

With all this conflicting and ambiguous information it is essential that there is an independent source of information about the state of the beaches. *The Reader's Digest Good Beach Guide* is exactly that. This book has been prepared by the Marine Conservation Society to give a clear, definitive guide to the state of beaches around the British Isles. The book will allow you, the reader, to make an informed choice about whether to bathe and where to bathe. Britain has thousands of beaches and, although we have not attempted to describe every one, details of over five hundred beaches are included in the guide. Of these beaches 71 are featured in detail as good beaches and are recommended places to visit. We all have a different idea of what makes a beach a good beach; however, the prime criterion for a beach to be featured in this book is water quality. If your favourite beach is not included in the guide, it may be that it is not monitored, or that monitoring has shown that the quality of the seawater is not satisfactory. A beautiful-looking beach may have dangerously high levels of viruses and bacteria in the water, and may be affected by sewage.

Sewage is not the only problem although it is the prime reason this book was written. The coast is also under pressure from housing, industry and fishing. Although development encroaches day by day, there are many areas around the British coast with some degree of protection. Britain has 38 stretches of Heritage Coast, unspoilt areas with a high scenic value. Although this is a definition rather than a statutory designation, there are specific management plans and policies for these sites to ensure their survival. There are many Areas of Outstanding Natural Beauty in coastal locations; protection of these areas is also through management plans or through special policies in local planning. In addition there are some statutory designations; numerous coastal Sites of Special Scientific Interest have been identified because of their

Development of many different kinds puts the coast under pressure.

flora, fauna or landscape features. These are managed through agreements with the nature conservation agencies of England, Scotland and Wales and potentially damaging operations can be restricted.

Many nature reserves on land have coastal sections and are managed to protect their environment and therefore the coast. The National Trust, through a project called

Lundy – one of only two statutory Marine Nature Reserves in Britain.

Enterprise Neptune, owns 853 km (530 miles) of coastline in England and Wales. Many of the beaches in this guide are either in the care or direct management of the Trust, or the land adjoining the beach is owned by the Trust and access for visitors has been improved. The Trust also manages conservation interests such as sand dune restoration or cliff grazing schemes to maintain habitats for coastal birds and other species.

The sites and reserves described are for the protection and management of land and coastal land. There is, in contrast, very little protection available for the area below the water. There are only two statutory Marine Nature Reserves in

Britain, in the waters around Lundy and Skomer. Both of these are small sites and their total area of protected marine environment is very small. These reserves were designated because they are in known special areas, but much more of the marine environment needs to be protected. Truly marine areas need protection as much as sites on land. Just because it is difficult to see the effect that we are having on the seabed doesn't mean that all is well. For example, trawling pressure in the North Sea has been likened to ploughing a field seven times a year with the same devastating effect.

A puffin – one of Britain's most charming coastal birds.

Not many of us get a chance to explore the seabed, but wherever we are we should be thoughtful and responsible when exploring the coast. Visitor pressure can disrupt shore life and lead to erosion of fragile ecosystems. When at the coast follow the Marine Conservation Society's Seashore Code: be careful at the coast, always keep an eye on the tide and be aware that the sea can be a very hostile environment. Show respect for the living creatures at the coast, take photos as souvenirs not living animals, don't drop litter, drive on roads not beaches and try to avoid disturbing wildlife.

'Take nothing but photographs,
leave nothing but footprints, waste nothing but time.'

CHAPTER TWO

HOW TO USE
THE READER'S DIGEST GOOD BEACH GUIDE

The best way to use this guide is to sit down with the book and to plan your holiday either around one of the featured beaches in the guide or one of the listed beaches with top-rated water quality and an adequate level of sewage treatment (a full explanation of sewage treatment and the implications on your health is given in Chapter 11). If you have already chosen where you are going, you can look up the beach in the book and then make the choice to swim or not to swim.

This chapter is a step-by-step guide explaining how to use the *Guide*. We have included a key to the water quality rating system used in the guide and an explanation of information presented in the tables.

The guide is divided into eight regional chapters, the South-West, the South-East, the East Coast, the North-West and the Isle of Man, Scotland, Wales, Northern Ireland, and the Channel Islands. Each regional chapter lists all the beaches identified under the EC Bathing Water Directive and some non-identified beaches (beaches that are identified under the Directive are in **bold** type). Most of the regions have featured beaches that we recommend people to visit since they have a high standard of water quality and a low probability of being contaminated with sewage.

The featured beaches in the *Guide* represent a selection of different types, ranging from the busier holiday resorts to quieter beaches off the beaten track. There are many entries in the tables that qualify for featured status on the basis of water quality. These have not been featured due to one of the following factors: a lack of information on the area, dangerous or restricted access to the site or adverse reports on management or littering.

The EC Bathing Water Directive

To be featured in the guide a beach has passed various microbiological standards laid down by the European Commission in the EC Bathing Water Directive (76/160/EEC). Since the EC Bathing Water Directive does not have a scientific base, and the microbiological standards set are arbitrary, this is not the only standard a beach must reach to be featured in the guide. The water quality rating system for *The Reader's Digest Good Beach Guide* has also taken into account the latest scientific research into bathing water quality and health. Recent events in Europe suggest that there will be extensive changes to the EC Water Bathing Directive with the possibility that the Directive may be strengthened and that water quality targets may be raised in response to recent scientific findings.

At present, under the EC Bathing Water Directive around four hundred and fifty bathing waters have been identified in the UK. These sites are regularly monitored throughout the bathing season, from May to September, by the National Rivers Authority (NRA) in England and Wales, the River Purification Boards (RPB) in Scotland, and the Department of the Environment in Northern Ireland. These authorities monitor for the number of coliform bacteria, faecal coliform bacteria and faecal streptococcus bacteria present in samples of seawater taken from identified bathing areas over the official bathing season, usually around twenty samples are taken. These bacteria are found in the gut of every person and are used as indicator species for sewage pollution. Faecal streptococcus bacteria can cause diseases in people, especially in cuts and wounds. Sewage may also carry enteric viruses and salmonella, hepatitis A virus and many other disease causing agents. The Directive does allow for the monitoring of enteric viruses and salmonella but since the Government bases its results only on the coliform and streptococcus counts, the Marine Conservation Society is limited to the use of this data.

There are two standards within the EC Bathing Water Directive: these are called the Mandatory Standards (also known as the Imperative or Minimum Standards) and the Guideline Standards which are twenty times stricter. The Mandatory Standards are the minimum legal standards that all Britain's identified bathing beaches should meet, the deadline for compliance being 1995. The EC Bathing Water Directive states that member states must comply with the Mandatory Standards and should strive to achieve the Guideline Standards. It is the Mandatory Standards that are referred to when a beach is given a pass or fail by the Department of the Environment. A beach which has been declared a pass by the Department of the Environment is not claiming to be sewage free – merely that the sewage has reached a certain dilution.

The Marine Conservation Society Water Quality Classes

The Marine Conservation Society divides the bathing water quality results into five water quality classes rather than the crude pass/fail used by the Department of the Environment. A full explanation of the water quality rating system follows. It should be noted that *The Reader's Digest Good Beach Guide* water quality rating system is a cumulative scale; for example, if a beach does not qualify for two dolphins it cannot qualify for the higher quality three dolphins and above.

---

f – fail

less than 95% pass of the Mandatory Standards

The Department of the Environment regard this as a fail. These beaches are heavily contaminated by sewage. The Marine Conservation Society would advise that these waters should not be used for bathing or any other water contact sports.

'Vote with your feet – don't swim here, this beach is polluted with sewage!'

---

one dolphin

95% pass of Mandatory Standards

The Department of the Environment regard this as a pass of the EC Bathing Water Directive, this is the minimum legal requirement for bathing beaches. The UK has promised that all bathing beaches will reach at least this 95% Mandatory Standard pass by 1995. These waters are, however, almost certainly contaminated by sewage and carry a significant health risk according to recent research carried out by the Water Research Centre. It should be noted that some beaches which have met this standard may be placed in the Guideline Standard pass category according to the Department of the Environment, since they will accept a 95% compliance with the Mandatory Standards coupled with the requirements for a Guideline pass as adequate for an overall Guideline pass. The Marine Conservation Society believe that this 95% compliance with the Mandatory Standards is inadequate, and will not recommend a beach in the *Guide* if it has failed the Mandatory Standards at any time over the bathing season.

'Vote with your feet – this bathing beach is only achieving bare minimum legal requirements.'

two dolphins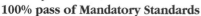
100% pass of Mandatory Standards
Although consistently passing the Mandatory Standards, research suggests that beaches with water of this quality may not be adequate to safeguard your health. Therefore, the Marine Conservation Society cannot recommend such beaches.

'The water is almost certainly affected by sewage.'

---

three dolphins
100% pass of Mandatory Standards
80% pass of Guideline Coliform Standards
This is the minimum standard that a beach must reach to be recommended in *The Reader's Digest Good Beach Guide*. Although faecal coliforms are no longer thought to be the most reliable standard for monitoring sewage pollution, the coliform counts for these bathing beaches suggest that there is very little sewage pollution.

'Come on in! The water's lovely.'

---

four dolphins
100% pass of Mandatory Standards
80 % pass of Guideline Coliform Standards
90 % pass of Guideline Faecal Streptococcus Standards
This bracket illustrates those beaches that will get near the standards for bathing water that should be our target.

'These waters should be the cleanest bathing areas in the UK.'

Come on in! The water's lovely.

Track Record

Most of the beaches in the guide, both the featured beaches and the listed beaches, have a track record. The track record shows how consistently the water quality has passed the Mandatory Standard at the beach. This is particularly useful for pinpointing those that have either failed or passed consistently over previous years.

For example, ☐☐☐☐☐|**✗**|**✓**|**✓**| would indicate that a beach passed the Mandatory Standard in 1993 and 1992, failed in 1991, and that no data was available before this time.

Sewage

The tables also give information on the amount of sewage discharged in the area, the degree of treatment the sewage has undergone prior to discharge and where the discharge point is relative to low water mean (all distances are given in metres unless otherwise stated). A full explanation of the different stages of sewage treatment is included in Chapter 11.

Abbreviations

NRA – National Rivers Authority
RPB – River Purification Board
DoE NI – Department of the Environment for Northern Ireland
UWWTD – Urban Waste Water Treatment Directive
LWM – low water mark
HWM – high water mark
UV – ultraviolet

Naturist beaches are usually clearly signposted.

In the tables and the index **bold** entries indicate beaches identified under the EC Bathing Waters Directive. EC identification of the featured beaches may be determined by the index entries.

Naturist Beaches

There are a growing number of specialist naturist beaches in Britain. It is important to note that some people may not wish to visit a naturist beach so the beach should be clearly signposted. The list below gives several beaches used by naturists in this country. If you wish to find out more about naturism contact the Central Council for British Naturism.

South-West:
Wild Pear Beach near Combe Martin, Devon
Polgaver Bay, Carlyon Bay, Cornwall
Pilchard Cove, Slapton Sands, Devon
Studland Beach (mid section), Dorset

South-East:
Brighton East Beach, Brighton, East Sussex
Fairlight Cove, Hastings, East Sussex
Long Rock Beach, Swalecliffe,

Whitestable, Kent
St Osyth, Essex
Holkham, Norfolk

East Coast:
Fraisthorpe Sands, Bridlington, North Humberside

Scotland:
Ardeer Beach, Stevenson, Ayrshire
Cleat's Shore, Lagg, Isle of Arran

SOUTH-WEST ENGLAND

THIS SECTION COVERS THE COAST FROM CLEVEDON IN AVON TO BOURNEMOUTH IN DORSET,
AND INCLUDES BEACHES ON THE ISLE OF WIGHT. THE COASTAL SCENERY RANGES FROM THE
HEAVILY INDUSTRIALISED COAST OF AVON TO THE BEAUTY OF THE SOUTH-WEST PENINSULA. THIS
CHAPTER ALSO INCLUDES SOME INFORMATION ON THE ISLES OF SCILLY, PART OF THE DUCHY OF
CORNWALL. SINCE NO BATHING WATER QUALITY INFORMATION IS AVAILABLE TO US WE HAVE
NOT FEATURED ANY INDIVIDUAL BEACHES ON THE ISLANDS.

•

There are hundreds of kilometres of glorious coastline along the south-west peninsula
and the south west coast has a very high number of bathing waters identified under
the EC Bathing Water Directive. Long sweeping bays and small secluded coves are
separated by rugged headlands. Spectacular rocky cliffs contrast with smooth turf slopes
where wild flowers abound. Some of Britain's loveliest unspoilt scenery is to be found
along this coast and many of the cleanest beaches and bathing waters are found in the
West Country.

The area is certainly not free of problems. Various forms of pollution affect several
beaches. Untreated sewage is discharged close inshore and is washed back on to the sands
at popular resorts. Croyde Bay in Devon is a privately owned beach affected by such
problems. The beach owner is taking legal action against the local water service company
over the state of the beach which is continually strewn with sewage related debris such as
sanitary towels and condoms. Both South West Water and Wessex Water have investment
programmes to deal with the sewage problems of the region, but there is still a very long
way to go. In the immediate future it appears that sewage is going to be an everyday
obstacle faced by the surfers at Newquay. In other areas, the china clay industry has
covered once pristine sands with a film of white dust and the Cornish tin mining industry
has been responsible for chronic and acute pollution by mine waste.

Congestion problems on small country roads can build up in the summer as large
numbers of tourists flock to the beaches. Long queues of traffic develop on the narrow
lanes and the picturesque fishing villages heave with cars. The beaches become crowded
and this can lead to damage with paths over dunes becoming badly eroded and littering
on otherwise beautiful areas. To avoid some of these problems go to the beach by public
transport or visit the area in the spring or autumn. Remember, in winter you can have
huge expanses of golden sand of the south west peninsula to yourself.

•

About 40km (25 miles) to the south-west of Land's End, in the track of the North
Atlantic Drift, lie the Isles of Scilly. The Isles of Scilly are the most westerly land of
Great Britain and comprise an archipelago of some two hundred granite islands and rocks
separated from each other and the mainland by a shallow sea. The climate is mild with
little variation in summer and winter temperatures. Many of the islands are small, devoid of
vegetation, but the five largest – St Mary's, St Martin's, Bryher, Tresco and St Agnes – are
inhabited and support farming, fishing and tourism industries and are marvellous places to
explore. Visitors to the Isles of Scilly are rewarded by beautiful scenery, shallow seas and a
fascinating insight into the islands' past.

LEFT: St Martin's, Isles of Scilly.

Rating	Resort	Sewage outlets	Population discharging from outlet	Type of treatment	Discharge point relative to LWM (Low Water Mark)	Remarks	Track record
	AVON						
	Clevedon						
	Bay					Water quality not monitored by NRA in 1993	✗✗✗✗✓✗✗
f	**Marine Lake** ST 398712	1	60,000	Fine screening, filtration, settlement and disinfection	At HWM	Rocks and mud. Crude discharges now removed. All flow to sewage treatment works at Kingston Seymour.	✗✗
	Weston-Super-Mare						
f	**Uphill Slipway** ST 312058						✓✓✗
f	Sanatorium ST314600						✗✓✗
f	**Tropicana** ST316607						✓✓✓
f	Grand Pier ST317615						✗✗✗
⌢⌢	Marine Lake					Improvement scheme completed 1990. Sandy. Rocks at north end of the beach. Main beaches cleaned mechanically and by hand over the summer on a daily basis.	✓✓✓
f	**Kewstoke Sand Bay (near Weston)** ST330635	1	75,000	Fine screening, disinfection	400m below LWM	Beach affected by sewage related debris, sewage and syringes reported summer 1993.	✓✗✓✓✓✓✗
	SOMERSET						
	Berrow						
⌢	**North** ST293545						✓✓✓
f	**South** ST290535					Sandy. Sewage related debris sometimes a problem.	✓✗✓✓✓✓✗
⌢	**Brean** ST296585					Sandy.	✓✓✓✓✓✓✓
	Burnham-on-Sea						
⌢	Yacht Club ST301480						✗✗✓
⌢	**Jetty** ST302488	1	36,000	Fine screening, filtration, settlement and disinfection	At HWM.	All flow to West Huntspill sewage treatment works. 1.5km stretch of beach gently shelving. Swimming and bathing is dangerous at most states of the tide. There is a ramp for disabled access. Beach cleaned daily by hand.	✗✓
	East Quantoxhead	1	800	Maceration	At LWM	Rocks and sand. Water quality not monitored by NRA in 1993.	
	Doniford	1	5,000	Fine screened	100m above LWM	Sand and mud. Water quality not monitored by NRA in 1993.	✗✓

Rating	Resort	Sewage outlets	Population discharging from outlet	Type of treatment	Discharge point relative to LWM (Low Water Mark)	Remarks	Track record
	Watchet	1	4,500	Raw	100m above LWM	Sand and mud. Water quality not monitored by NRA in 1993	✗✓
🐦🐦	**Blue Anchor** ST023435					Sand and shingle. Flows to Minehead headworks.	✓✗✓✓✓✗✓✓
	Dunster						
🐦	**North West** SS997455						✓✓✓
	South East SS997455					Sand and shingle. Flows to Minehead headworks. Water quality not monitored by NRA in 1993.	✗✗✗✗✓✓✓
	Minehead						
🐦🐦	**Terminus** SS973465						✓✓✓
🐦🐦	The Strand SS978463	1	35,000	Screening and disinfection	Long sea outfall & tidal discharge 750m below LWM	Sandy. Headworks and outfall completed 1989.	✓✓✓
	Porlock Bay						
🐦🐦 🐦🐦	**Porlock Weir** SS864479	3	850 1,200 450	Raw Raw Raw	At LWM At LWM At LWM	Pebbles.	✓✗✓✓✓✓✓✓
	NORTH DEVON						
f	**Lynmouth** SS725497	1	4,300	Raw	110m below	Pebbles. New full treatment works and outfall planned for 1995.	✗✗✓✗✗✗✓✗
🐦	**Combe Martin** SS577473	1	3,600	Raw	65m below	Pebbles and sand. New full treatment works and 0.5km outfall planned by 1995.	✗✗✗✗✓✗✗✓
	Ilfracombe						
🐦	**Hele Beach** SS535479						✗✗✓
f	**Capstone Beach** SS518479						✗✗✓✓✓✓✗✗
🐦🐦	Tunnels SS514478	2	22,000 744	Raw Raw	235m below 30m below	Sandy. Improvements planned to include full treatment works and medium sea outfall by 1995.	✓✓✓
	Rockham Bay					Rocky. Water quality not monitored by NRA in 1993.	
	Barricane Bay					Sandy cove surrounded by rocks. Water quality not monitored by NRA in 1993.	

1. WOOLACOMBE SAND, WOOLACOMBE, DEVON

OS ref: SS4500

Two rugged headlands, Morte Point and Baggy Point, bound this magnificent, straight, west-facing beach. Three kilometres (a mile and a quarter) of flat sands extend south from the rocky shore at Woolacombe. This beach has achieved the highest grading possible for its water quality in the *Guide*. The 350m (380 yard) wide sands are backed by a narrow belt of dunes, behind which rise the shrub covered slopes of Woolacombe Down. Woolacombe Sand is popular with surfers, because of the waves that wash the shore, and with families wanting to relax on the beach. After building sand castles and exploring the rock pools you can escape from the crowds by taking a stroll on the headland. On the northern side of Woolacombe there is a pocket sized beach in complete contrast to the long sweeping sands to the south. The small sandy Barricane beach nestles within the rocky shore stretching to Morte Point and is overlooked by the hotels and guest houses of Woolacombe.

Water quality

There is one sewage discharge in the area, discharging secondary treated sewage from 13,200 people 100m (110 yards) below low water mark.

Bathing safety

It is dangerous to swim near the rocks or at low tide because of undertow currents. Lifeguards patrol Woolacombe from Whitsun to the second week in September.

Access

A turning off the approach road to Woolacombe from the B3231 leads to car parks behind the beach.

Parking

There are several car parks behind the dunes which provide over 1,000 spaces.

Public transport

From Mondays to Saturdays there is a bus (number 308) from Barnstaple to Woolacombe.

Toilets

There are toilets in the car park behind the dunes.

Food

There are cafés and shops at Woolacombe.

Seaside activities

Swimming, surfing, windsurfing, diving, sailing and fishing. Surfboards are available for hire. Hang gliding from Woolacombe Down.

Wildlife and walks

The South West Coast Path leads in both directions from Morte Bay. The gorse-clad Baggy Point affords excellent views across the bay, as does the jagged slate headland of Morte Point. On a clear day you can see Lundy Island lying 24km (15 miles) away in the Bristol Channel. The waters around this island are a Marine Nature Reserve renowned for the rich marine wildlife around its rocky shores. The steep cliffs that soar 120m (390ft) above the sea are the haunt of numerous seabirds. Trips to the island to explore its superb shore in greater detail are available from Ilfracombe harbour.

Track record

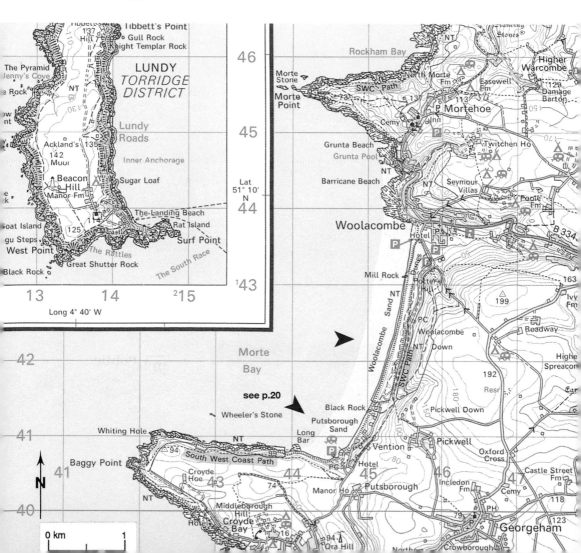

2. PUTSBOROUGH BEACH, WOOLACOMBE, DEVON

OS ref: SS4500

Situated at the northern end of Baggy Point and the southern end of Woolacombe Sands, this beach is ideal for families as the headland shelters the beach on most occasions. The beach is especially popular with surfers when other beaches along the coast are blown out.

Water quality

There is no sewage discharged in the vicinity of this beach.

Bathing safety

It is generally safe to bathe here but be aware that there is not full lifeguard cover.

Access

From Croyde or Georgeham along a minor road to a private car park.

Parking

There is a private car park right above the beach.

Public transport

From Mondays to Saturdays there is a bus (number 308) from Barnstaple to Woolacombe.

Toilets

There are toilets at the car park.

Food

There is a small gift shop that

also has take away food and an ice-cream counter.

🏄 Seaside activities

Swimming, surfing and shore fishing. There are surfboards available for hire. There is also rock climbing on Baggy Point which is a good spectator sport.

🌼 Wildlife and walks

The South-West Coast Path runs behind the beach. There are several footpaths over Baggy Point, much of which is owned by the National Trust. The headland is a Site of Special Scientific Interest because of its geology which is of national importance. The area is particularly colourful in late spring and early summer when coastal wildflowers smother the lower cliffs. Birdwatching is also well rewarded here and the occasional sighting of a grey seal, dolphin or porpoise is to be expected in the summer.

➤ **For map position see p.19**

Rating	Resort	Sewage outlets	Population discharging from outlet	Type of treatment	Discharge point relative to LWM (Low Watter Mark)	Remarks	Track record
↷	**Croyde Bay** SS434393	1	6,400	Fine screening	Below LWM	Strong undertow. Lifeguards. Problems with sewage-related debris.	✓✓✓✓✓✓✓
↷	**Saunton Sands** SS445376					Sand. Lifeguards. Affected by marine litter including sewage-related debris.	✓✓✓✓✓✓✓
f	**Instow** SS471304	1	8,500	Fine screening	Pumped discharge at LWM	Polluted by Rivers Taw and Torridge. Uprated sewage works construction under way, due for completion in 1997.	✗✗✗✓✗✗✗✗
↷	**Westward Ho!** SS432294	1	4,600	Fine screening	10m below	Improvements as above.	✓✓✓✓✓✓✓
	Clovelly	1	1,300	Raw	At LWM	Water quality not monitored by NRA in 1993.	
	Shipload Bay					Water quality not monitored by NRA in 1993.	☐☐☐☐☐✓✓☐
↷↷ ↷↷	**Hartland Quay**					Rocks, boulders, pebbles and stunning rock formations.	✓✓✓✓✓✓✓
	Welcombe Mouth					Water quality not monitored by NRA in 1993.	
	CORNWALL						
↷	**Bude Sandy Mouth** SS202099					Sandy. Lifeguards in holiday season. Although this beach fulfills the Guideline pass of the EC Bathing Water directive it has failed the Mandatory Standard at some stage over the season and so cannot be recommended.	☐☐☐☐☐✓✓✓
↷	**Bude Crooklets** SS203072					Sandy. Surf bathing.	✗✗✗✓✓✗✓✓
f	**Bude Summerleaze** SS204066	1	12,700	Primary	1,000 m below LWM	New inland treatment works and outfall opened summer 1992.	☐☐☐☐☐✗✓✗

3. WIDEMOUTH SAND, WIDEMOUTH BAY, CORNWALL

OS ref: SS1902

In contrast to a lot of the beaches in North Cornwall, the 1.5km (1,600 yards) of flat sands at Widemouth Bay is backed by low cliffs and undulating grassy fields which stretch down to the beach from the whitewashed houses of Widemouth village. Flat rocks, which can become too hot to lie on, stretch away in either direction from this popular surfing beach. The relatively easy access, which can be so important if you do not wish to negotiate steep cliff paths, unfortunately means that in summer the beach often becomes very congested. The cliffs that rise on either side of the beach provide walks away from the busy sands.

Water quality

No sewage is discharged in the vicinity of this beach.

Litter

There are reports of marine litter being washed up on this beach. The beach is cleaned all year round by the local authority and there is a dog ban.

Bathing safety

Surf bathing is dangerous at low tide, and beware of currents near the rocks at each side of the beach. Lifeguards patrol the beach during the summer.

Access

Widemouth Bay is signposted from the A39 south of Bude. Sandy slopes and steps lead from the car parks on to the beach.

Parking

There are two car parks behind the beach at either end of the bay with spaces for approximately 200 cars.

Public transport

The nearest station is at Umberleigh about 35km (22 miles) away and there are 5 local bus services a day from Bude.

Toilets

There are toilets at the car parks.

Food

There is a café at the southern car park and a beach shop at the northern car park.

Seaside activities

Swimming, surfing, windsurfing and fishing. Surfboards are available for hire.

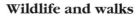

Wildlife and walks

The coast path leads off the road south of the beach, climbing Penhalt Cliff towards Dizzards Point. There are superb views looking back along the straight coast stretching north of Bude.

Track Record

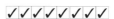

Rating	Resort	Sewage outlets	Population discharging from outlet	Type of treatment	Discharge point relative to LWM (Low Water Mark)	Remarks	Track record
f	Crackington Haven SX142969					Lifeguards, reduced cover from 1 July to August Bank Holiday. Dog ban. Good walking area.	✔✘✘
	Boscastle	1	1,300	Raw	At LWM remote from harbour	Harbour outfall inaccessible. Water quality not monitored by NRA in 1993.	
	Tintagel	1	1,500	Raw	At LWM	Water quality not monitored by NRA in 1993.	
f	Trebarwith Strand SX048863					Swimming can be dangerous. Lifeguards during holiday season.	✔✔✘
	Port Isaac	1	1,800	Secondary	At LWM	Water quality not monitored by NRA in 1993.	
⌢	**Polzeath** SW936792	1	1,700	Screening and septic tank treatment	Pulse discharge on ebbing tide at LWM	Cleaned year round. Dog ban. Bathing can be dangerous at low water. Lifeguards. Transfer to inland treatment works for 1994. Although this beach fulfills the requirements for a guideline pass of the EC Bathing Water Directive it has failed the Mandatory Standard at some stage over the season and so cannot be recommended.	✔✔✔✔✔✔✔
⌢⌢	**Daymer Bay** SW928776					Sandy.	✔✔✔✔✔✔✔
⌢	**Rock Beach** SW927758					Swimmers beware currents. Good sailing. Sandy.	✘✘✔✔✔✔✔
⌢	Padstow SW919764	1	3,800	Fine screening		No swimming. Transfer to inland treatment works planned for 1995.	
f	**Trevone Bay** SW892761	1	1,000	Raw	At LWM	Bathing can be dangerous. Lifeguards. Transfer to inland treatment works planned for 1995.	✘✘✘✔✔✘✔✘
⌢	**Harlyn Bay** SW877755	1	4,900	Secondary	At LWM	Lifeguards in holiday season. Beach cleaned all year. Transfer to inland treatment works planned for 1995.	✔✔✔✔✔✔✔
⌢⌢ ⌢⌢	**Mother Ivey's Bay** SW863760					Pedestrian access. Sandy.	✔✔✔✔✔✔✔

4. CONSTANTINE BAY, TREYARNON, CORNWALL

OS ref: SW8676

This wide, sweeping arc of gently shelving soft pale sands, backed by large Marram-covered dunes and bounded on either side by low headlands with rocky outcrops stretching seaward, is a picture to behold. There is very limited parking and there are few facilities available at the beach. The beach is cleaned all year round.

Water quality

There is no sewage discharged in the vicinity of this beach.

Bathing safety

Bathing is dangerous near the rocks. Lifeguards patrol from Whitsun to August Bank Holiday.

Access

Off the B3276.

Parking

There is space for 200 cars off the B3276 two minutes away from the beach.

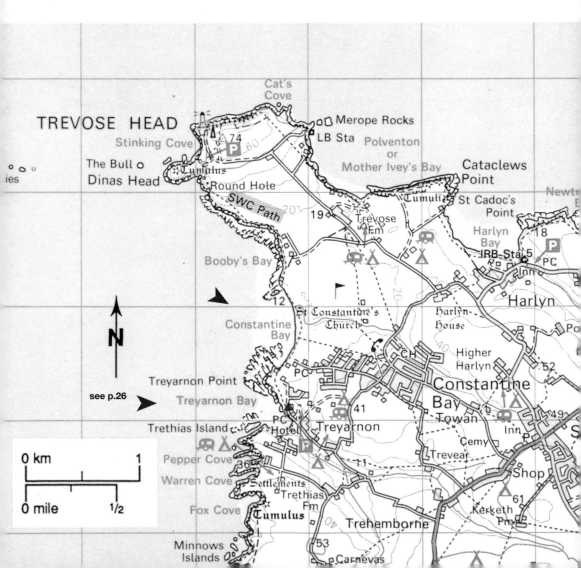

 Public transport
The nearest station is Bodmin Parkway. There are infrequent buses to Constantine Bay.

 Toilets
There are toilets at the entrance to the beach.

 Food
There is none available.

 Seaside activities
Swimming and surfing.

Wildlife and walks
The dunes behind the beach are under restoration, with Marram grass being planted to stabilise the sands. There are interesting rock pools to explore. The coast path skirts the bay but the low cliffs do not provide the spectacular views that are found elsewhere along this coast.

Track record

5. TREYARNON BAY, PADSTOW, CORNWALL

OS ref: SW8574

Treyarnon is a wide sandy bay in an Area of Outstanding Natural Beauty next to the larger Constantine Bay. The beach is very popular with surfers, but please note that swimming is dangerous near the cliffs and surfing is dangerous at low tide.

Water quality

 Litter
The beach is cleaned regularly and dogs are banned.

Bathing safety
Swimmers should keep to the centre of the beach. Lifeguards patrol the beach from Whitsun to August Bank Holiday. There is a natural pool in the rocks providing safe swimming at low tide.

 Access
Turn off the B3276 to get to Treyarnon.

 Parking
Car park adjacent to the beach with approximately 150 places.

WC Toilets
There are toilets near the beach including facilities for disabled visitors.

 Food
Beach shop and hotel.

 Seaside activities
Swimming, surfing. There are surf boards available for hire.

 Wildlife and walks
Treyarnon is on the North Cornwall Coast Path which has some spectacular views.

Track record

✓✓✓✓✓✓✓

➤ For map position see p.24

Rating	Resort	Sewage outlets	Population discharging from outlet	Type of treatment	Discharge point relative to LWM (Low Water Mark)	Remarks	Track record
f	**Mawgan Porth** SW848674					Surfing dangerous at low tide. Improvements planned to construct reed bed treatment system at St Columb. Major sewage treatment works by 1994. Sandy.	✗✗✓✗✗✗✓✗
	Bedruthan Steps					Steps to beach closed, access dangerous and bathing dangerous.	
⌢⌢	**Watergate Bay** SW841649					Sandy	✓✓✓✓✓✗✓✓
⌢	Porth Beach SW829627					Sandy. Lifeguards. Flows have been transferred to main Newquay system.	✗✓✓
	Newquay Bay						
⌢⌢	**Towan Beach** SW810620	1	50,000	Maceration/ screening		Pumped discharge 75m below LWM Lifeguards. Improvements planned. Possible interim fine screening ahead of main treatment works required to meet the UWWTD for 2,000.	✓✓✓✓✓✓✓✓
⌢⌢ ⌢⌢	**Fistral Beach** SW796623					Strong currents when rough. Lifeguards.	✓✓✓✓✓✓✓
⌢⌢	**Crantock** SW784608					Swimming dangerous at low water and near Gannel estuary. Lifeguards.	✓✓✓✓✓✓✓
⌢⌢	**Holywell Bay** SW765595					Surfing dangerous at low tide. Lifeguards. Sandy.	✓✓✓
	Perranporth						
⌢⌢ ⌢⌢	Penhale Village SW762570						✓✓✓
⌢	**Village End Beach** SW757548	1	12,000	Maceration	At LWM	Dangerous at low tide. Lifeguards. New full treatment works planned for 1995.	✗✓✓
f	**Trevaunance Cove** SW723517	1	4,000	Fine screening	Pumped outfall at LWM	Sandy. Powerful surf. Improvements planned for new full treatment works, new outfall, re-sewerage and new pumping station planned for 1995.	✗✗✓✓✓✗✗✗
⌢⌢ ⌢⌢	**Porthtowan Sandy** SW691481					Surfing dangerous at low water. Lifeguards. Sewage related debris problem.	✓✓✓✓✓✓✓
⌢⌢ ⌢⌢	**Portreath** SW653455	1	26,300	Fine screening	At LWM east of village	Swimming dangerous near pier. Lifeguards. Improvements planned to construct full sewage treatment works and re-sewerage by the year 2000 to meet the UWWTD.	✓✓✓✓✓✓✓
	Deadman's Cove (Cambourne)	1	19,500	Raw	At LWM	Water quality not monitored by NRA in 1993. Improvements planned to construct full sewage treatment works and resewerage by the year 2000 to meet UWWTD.	

6. THE TOWANS, HAYLE, ST IVES, CORNWALL

OS ref: SW5639

St Ives has a magnificent necklace of golden beaches, backed on its southern edge by high dunes and some rocky outcrops. The approach to the beach at Hayle is uninspiring as there is much development on the landward side of the dunes. The beach however is lovely, 5km (3 miles) of pale rippled sands fringed with dunes and rocky outcrops. Dogs are banned from the beach from Easter to October.

Water quality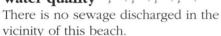
There is no sewage discharged in the vicinity of this beach.

 Litter
The beach is cleaned regularly.

Bathing safety
There are strong currents around the river mouth which make bathing dangerous. Lifeguards patrol the beach in the summer.

Sand dunes at Hayle.

Access
The beach is signposted from the A30 through Hayle. The road leads up to the car parks behind the dunes and the sands are no more than five minutes walk.

P Parking
Car parks behind the dunes have plenty of spaces.

Public transport
The nearest station is at Hayle and there is an hourly bus service to the Towans in the summer.

WC Toilets
There are toilets at the car parks.

Food
There is a beach shop and cafés at the car parks.

Seaside activities
Swimming and surfing. Surfboards are available for hire.

Wet weather alternative
Hayle Paradise Park.

Wildlife and walks
Following the beach north brings you to the rocky shore towards

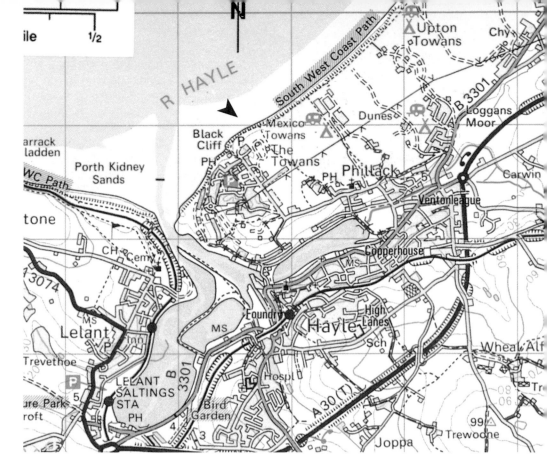

Godrevy Point where the coast path leads along the cliffs to Navax Point. There are some lovely views to take in across St Ives Bay.

Track record

| | | | | | ✓ | ✓ | ✓ | |

Rating	Resort	Sewage outlets	Population discharging from outlet	Type of treatment	Discharge point relative to LWM (Low Water Mark)	Remarks	Track record
⌒⌒	**Towans/Godrevy** SW581417					Sandy. Surfing. Swimming dangerous at low water. Lifeguards.	✓✓✓✓✓✓✓
	Carbis Bay						
⌒⌒ ⌒⌒	**Porth Kidney Sands** SW540385						☐☐☐☐☐☐✗✓✓
⌒⌒ ⌒⌒	**Station Beach** SW528389					Sandy and sheltered.	☐☐☐☐☐✓✓✓
	St Ives						
⌒	**Porthminster** SW522402					Sandy. Sheltered. Well managed beach.	✓✓✓✗✓✓✓✓
f	**Porthgwidden** SW522411					Sandy beach. All discharges ceased.	✗✓✗✗✗✗✓✗

7. PORTHMEOR, ST IVES, CORNWALL

OS ref: SW5141

The delightful old buildings which are crowded together on the narrow streets around the harbour spill directly on to the beach at Porthmeor. A row of stone houses faces on to the sands but they in no way spoil this most attractive of beaches. Below St Ives Head, also known as the Island, a kilometre (1,100 yards) of soft sand backed by low cliffs stretches west. Unlike the more sheltered beaches on the other side of the headland, Porthmeor is a surfer's beach with the waves from the Atlantic rolling on to the shore. A promenade at the foot of the cliffs provides all the facilities needed for a day on this lovely beach. St Ives is famous for its quality of light which has made it popular with artists, a fact reflected in the numerous art galleries and craft workshops to be found in the town. Dogs are banned from the beach from Easter until 1 October.

Water quality

There is one outfall serving 50 people which discharges fine screened sewage into the sea 150m (160 yards) from the harbour wall. There is an improvement scheme to transfer flows for full treatment near Hayle for 1995.

Litter

The beach is cleaned daily during the summer.

Bathing safety

Care must be taken when bathing during out-going tides, as there is an undertow. Patrolled by lifeguards in summer. An area for use of surfboards is marked with buoys.

Access

The beach is signposted within the town but it is best to use the large car park above the town and walk down to the beach. There are steps and a lane down on to the sands.

Parking

The main car park for the town is signposted on the

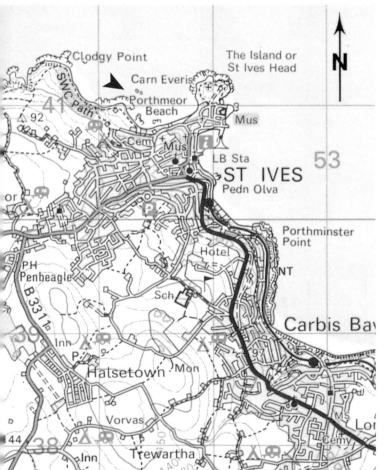

approach roads. There are car parks at either end of the beach; each has space for about 40 cars.

 Public transport
The nearest station is at St Ives which is only a short walk away.

 Toilets
There are toilets at the car parks.

 Food
There is a beach shop and café on the promenade.

 Seaside activities
Swimming and surfing. Deck chairs, surfboards and beach huts are available for hire. Boat trips around St Ives Bay are available from the harbour.

 Wet weather alternatives
Art galleries, craft workshops, Barbara Hepworth Museum, St Ives museum, St Ives Leisure and Squash Club.

 Wildlife and walks
From the beach a coastal path leads west along the low rocky cliffs to a series of sandy and rocky coves.

Track record

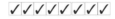

Rating	Resort	Sewage outlets	Population discharging from outlet	Type of treatment	Discharge point relative to LWM (Low Watter Mark)	Remarks	Track record
↝	St Just Priest's Cove SW772604					Shingle. Although this beach fulfills the requirements for a Guideline pass of the EC Bathing Water Directive it has failed the Mandatory Standard at some stage over the season and so cannot be recommended.	

harbour. There have been some complaints of sewage slicks in the bay in the past.

Litter
The local authority manages the cleaning up of litter on a regular basis.

Bathing safety
Bathing and surfing are safe at the southern end of the bay. Lifeguards patrol the beach during the summer months.

8. WHITESAND BAY, SENNEN COVE, CORNWALL

OS ref: SW3626

On the rugged Land's End Peninsula the splendid sweep of Whitesand Bay is in sharp contrast to the many rocky coves that indent the cliffs. From the picturesque little harbour of Sennen Cove the beach stretches north 1.5km (1 mile) to Aire Point, with steep cliffs ringing the northern section. The southern end of this moderately shelving beach is good for swimming and surfing, being sheltered by offshore reefs. The northern end is open to the full force of the Atlantic and conditions can be wild and dangerous. Dogs are banned from the beach between Easter and 1 October.

Water quality
There is one outfall serving 1,489 people that discharges macerated sewage at low water mark by the

Access
A road from the A30 to Land's End leads steeply down to Sennen Cove. There is easy access to the beach.

Parking
There is a car park in Sennen Cove and another on the approach road.

Public transport
The nearest station is at Penzance, there is a regular bus service in summer.

Toilets
There are toilets in the village.

Food
There are shops, cafés and a pub in the village.

Seaside activities
Swimming, surfing and angling. Fishing trips are available from the harbour. Surfboards can be hired.

Rating	Resort	Sewage outlets	Population discharging from outlet	Type of treatment	Discharge point relative to LWM (Low Water Mark)	Remarks	Track record
⌃⌃	**Porthcurno** SW387223	1	200	Maceration	At LWM	Sandy.	✓✓✓✓✓✓✓✓
	Lamorna Cove	1		Tidal tank	At LWM	Sand and rocks. Water quality not monitored by NRA in 1993.	
f	Mousehole SW470263	1	2,000	Raw	At LWM	Fishing port. Transfer to upgraded treatment works at Hayle and outfall planned for 1995.	
	Marazion and Mounts Bay:						
f	**Wherrytown** SW467294						✗✗✗
f	**Heliport** SW485311						✗✓✗
f	**Penzance** SW475298						✗✗✗✗✗✗✗✗
f	**Little Hogus** SW513310	12	37,585	Raw	11 at LWM, 1 at 50 below LWM	Sand/shingle. Scheme under construction to provide interception, pumping and transfer to Hayle for full treatment, completion due by 1995.	✓✓✗
⌃⌃ ⌃⌃	**Perran Sands** SW539293	1	1,000	Raw	At LWM	Sandy.	✓✓✓✓✓✗✓✓

 ## Wildlife and walks

The granite cliffs south from Sennen Cove to Land's End are owned by the National Trust. The coast path follows the cliff top which can be wild and windswept. It is probably the best way to approach Land's End avoiding the severe summer congestion of the most westerly tip of Britain, which has been rather spoilt by uncontrolled development.

Track record

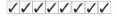
✓✓✓✓✓✓✓✓

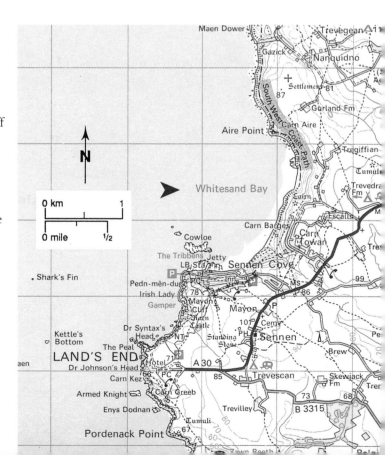

9. PRAA SANDS, ASHTON, HELSTON, CORNWALL

OS ref: GR5827

This is a particularly attractive sweep of sand between two rocky headlands and is popular with families. Sheltered by Hoe Point cliffs to the west the 1.5km (1 mile) sandy strip edged by high dunes stretches east to Lesceave Cliff and the granite Rinsey Headland. At low water around 100m (110 yards) of gently sloping sand is exposed with rockpools at either end of the beach. There are caravan parks nearby which make the beach busy.

Water quality

Litter
The beach is regularly cleaned by the National Trust but seaborne litter is frequently washed up.

Bathing safety
Bathing at low tide is very unsafe due to a rip current. The beach is patrolled by lifeguards in summer.

Access

Praa Sands is signposted from the A394 between Helston and Penzance. From the car park there is a short walk to the beach.

Parking

On the road down to the beach there is a car park with 100 spaces. There is another car park at the bottom of the hill.

Public transport

The nearest station is at Penzance with an hourly bus service.

Toilets

There are toilets at the entrance to the beach.

Food

Café and takeaways at the entrance to the beach.

Seaside activities

Swimming, diving, surfing, windsurfing, sailing, raft racing and fishing.

Wildlife and walks

The coast path from the eastern end of the beach leads away from the often crowded sands up Lesceave Cliff and on to Rinsey Head. Wheal Prosper, the engine house of an old copper mine stands on the headland; the property and the surrounding land is owned by the National Trust. The mine shaft has been capped and the building restored.

Track record

✓✓✓✓✓✓✓

Rating	Resort	Sewage outlets	Population discharging from outlet	Type of treatment	Discharge point relative to LWM (Low Watter Mark)	Remarks	Track record
f	**Porthleven West** SW632253	1	3,500	Raw	50m below LWM	Flint and pebbles. Bathing dangerous. Inland treatment works, pumping station, resewerage and tertiary treatment with discharge at harbour entrance planned for 1995.	✗✗✗✓✗✗✓✗

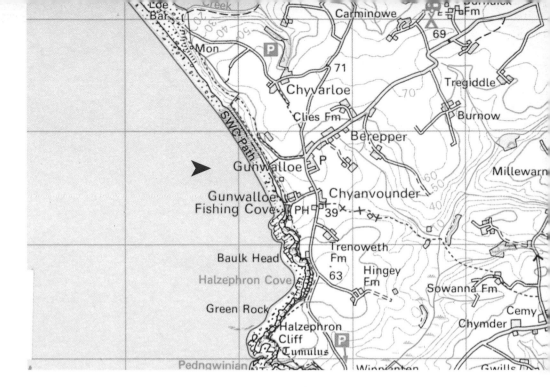

10. GUNWALLOE COVE, CORNWALL

OS ref: SW6322

Gunwalloe is a large beach that is mainly covered at high tide. There is a sandy cove to the north of the main beach. The National Trust owns much of the land in the area, a leaflet with further information is available from the National Trust. Dogs are banned from the beach.

Water quality

Litter
The beach is cleaned regularly by the National Trust.

Access
From Porthleven. There is easy sloping access suitable for wheelchairs.

Parking
There is parking available around 150m (160 yards) from the beach.

Public transport
It is difficult to get to the beach by public transport.

Toilets
There are toilets at the beach but no facilities for disabled visitors.

Food
There are cafés in the area.

Seaside activities
Swimming, surfing and fishing.

Wildlife and walks
There are many walks in the area. A walks pack is available from Kerrier District Council.

Track record

Rating	Resort	Sewage outlets	Population discharging from outlet	Type of treatment	Discharge point relative to LWM (Low Watter Mark)	Remarks	Track record
↶	**Poldhu Cove** SW665198					This sandy cove is a good starting point for reaching quieter coves to the north and south. Lifeguards in summer, bathing dangerous at low tide.	✔✔✔✔✔✔✔✔
↶↶	**Polurrian Cove** SW668187	1	1,600	Macerated	Pumped discharge at LWM	Sandy. Weekend lifeguards.	✔✔✔✔✔✔✔✔
	Kynance Cove					Sandy, safe bathing. A leaflet with further information on the area is available from the National Trust. Water quality not monitored by the NRA in 1993.	

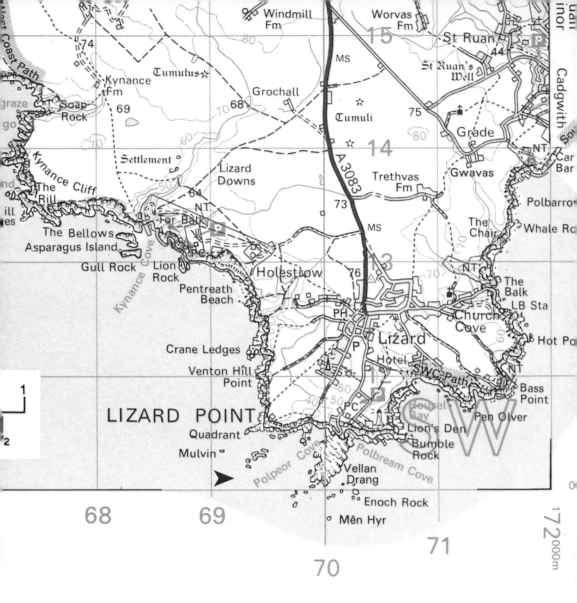

11. POLPEOR, THE LIZARD, CORNWALL

OS ref: SW7012

The Lizard Peninsula is beautiful and remote, with much of interest for the naturalist. Unfortunately in the summer it is overwhelmed by visitors and the narrow roads become congested with traffic. If you want to appreciate the lovely coves around the headland, make your visit early or late in the season to avoid some of the crowds. Polpeor is a small rock and shingle cove at the southernmost tip of the Lizard, framed by the cliffs of the Lizard Head and the Lizard Point, a rocky promontory that shelters the beach. The beach is 100m (110 yards) long and is completely covered at high water. A former lifeboat house and slipway adjoins the beach on to which a few boats are still drawn. The turning of the local marble-like serpentine rock has become a small local industry.

Water quality
No sewage is discharged in the vicinity of this beach.

 Bathing safety
It is safe to bathe in this area.

 Access
There is a 450m (490 yard) path from the car park to the beach.

 Parking
There are two car parks near the beach.

 Toilets
At the beach.

 Food
There are several cafés close to the beach.

 Seaside activities
Swimming and fishing.

 Wet weather alternatives
Museum of Cornish History in the village; lighthouse and lifeboat house open to the public.

Wildlife and walks
Several rare species of plant flourish in the warm climate of the Lizard Peninsula, particularly those of the maritime heathland which is a feature of the area.

Track record
No track record is available for this beach.

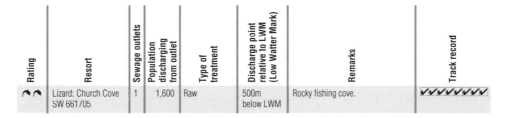

Rating	Resort	Sewage outlets	Population discharging from outlet	Type of treatment	Discharge point relative to LWM (Low Watter Mark)	Remarks	Track record
⌢⌢	Lizard: Church Cove SW 661705	1	1,600	Raw	500m below LWM	Rocky fishing cove.	✓✓✓✓✓✓✓✓

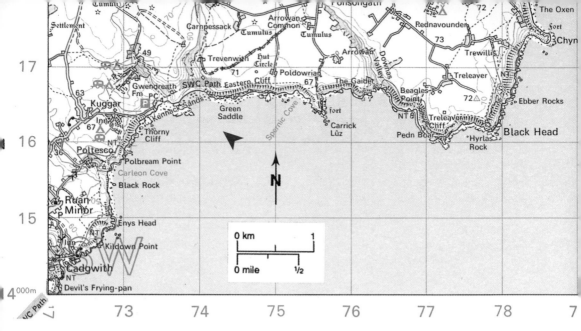

12. KENNACK SANDS, KUGGAR, CORNWALL

OS ref: SW7316

Probably the best swimming beach on the Lizard; Kennack is famous for its silver sands. Two separate 500m (550 yard) beaches merge at low tide to form one wide, gently sloping sandy beach. The pale sands, on the sheltered eastern side of the Lizard Peninsula, are fringed by dunes. At either end of the bay the sand gives way to shingle, which is bounded landward by cliffs. This is a popular family beach.

Water quality

No sewage is discharged in the vicinity of this beach.

Litter
Sometimes affected by marine litter on the beach.

Bathing safety
Bathing is safe.

Access
A road from Kuggar village signposted for Kennack ends behind the beach; there is a short walk through dunes to the sands.

Parking
There is a car park at the beach entrance with 250 spaces.

Toilets
There is a toilet in the car park.

Food
There are cafés at the entrance to the beach.

Seaside activities
Swimming, surfing, diving, windsurfing and fishing. Surfboards are available for hire next to the beach.

Wildlife and walks
The Cornwall South Coast Path proceeds east from the beach along the cliff tops towards Black Head with good sea views.

Track record
 ✓✓✓✓✓✓✓

Rating	Resort	Sewage outlets	Population discharging from outlet	Type of treatment	Discharge point relative to LWM (Low Watter Mark)	Remarks	Track record
↷↷	**Coverack** SW783186	1	800	Primary	100m below	Sand and shingle.	✔✔✔✔✔✔✔
↷↷ ↷↷	**Porthoustock** SW807217					Shingle with sand at low tide.	✔✔✔✔✔✔✔
f	**Porthallow** SW797233		100	Raw/septic tanks		Grey stones. Private discharges to be intercepted and treated on receipt of first time sewer requisition.	✘✘✘✘✔✘✔✘
f	**Maen Porth** SW790296 **Falmouth**					Sand and shingle. Lifeguards.	✔✘✔✔✔✔✔✘
f	**Swanpool Beach** SW790233	2	36,500	Maceration.	At LWM and 50m below LWM	Sand and shingle. Full treatment works and resewerage planned for 1995.	✔✘✔✔✔✔✘✘
↷	**Gyllyngvase** SW809316					Sandy. Lifeguards. Although this beach fulfils the requirements for a Guideline pass of the EC Bathing Water Directive it has failed the Mandatory Standard at some stage over the season and so cannot be recommended.	✔✘✔✔✔✔✔✔
↷	Feock: Loe Beach SW826320					Sand and shingle. Boating beach.	✔✔✔
	St Mawes	1	1,500	Secondary	100m below	Sandy. Safe swimming. Water quality not monitored by NRA in 1993.	
	St Anthony's Head					Sheltered bay; fine shingle at low tide. Water quality not monitored by NRA in 1993.	
	Towan Beach					Sand/rock. Beach owned and managed by the National Trust. An excellent starting point for walks. Water quality not monitored by NRA in 1993.	
	Portscatho	2	1,988 52	Raw Raw	At LWM At LWM	Sand and rock. Water quality not monitored by the NRA in 1993.	
	Porthcurnick Beach					Sand, some rocks. Water quality not monitored by NRA in 1993.	
↷↷	**Pendower Beach** SW898381					Sand and rock.	✔✔✔
↷↷ ↷↷	Carne Beach SW905383						✔✔
f	Portloe SW938394	2	200	Maceration	Pumped discharge at LWM	Sand and rock. Fishing village.	
	Portholland Beach					Shingle; sand at low tide. Old lime kilns on the shore.	
↷	**Porthluney Cove** SW973413					Sandy.	✔✔✔
	Hemmick Beach					Small, sandy bay. Water quality not monitored by NRA in 1993.	

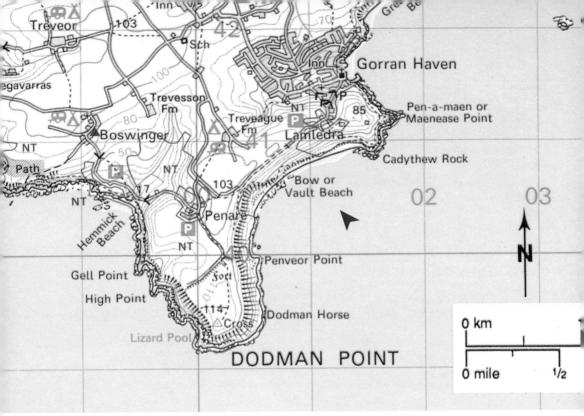

DODMAN POINT

0 km

0 mile   1/2

N

13. BOW OR VAULT BEACH, GORRAN HAVEN, CORNWALL

OS ref: SX0141

Sheltered on the eastern side of Dodman Point is the superb Vault Beach, a sweep of sand and shingle below steep, bracken and heather clad cliffs. From Maenease Point the beach curves for 1km (1,100 yards) to the rock outcrop of Penover Point. The cliffs rise to an impressive 110m (360ft) at Dodman Point.

Water quality

There is one sewage outfall discharging macerated sewage from 2,000 people on the north side of Maenease Head.

 Litter
A small amount on this beach.

Bathing safety
Bathing is safe with care.

Access
Follow the coast path south from Gorran Haven to reach a steep path down the cliffs.

 Parking
There is a National Trust car park at Lamledra Farm above the beach or at Penare.

WC Toilets
None.

Food
No food is available in the immediate vicinity.

Seaside activities
Swimming.

Wildlife and walks

The coast path along the cliff top leads on to Dodman Point; there is evidence of an Iron Age fort with a ditch and bank. At the point, a granite cross stands as a memorial to all the ships that have been wrecked on it.

There are marvellous views along much of the Cornish coast.

Track record

✓ ✗ ✓ ✓ ✓ ✓ ✓

Rating	Resort	Sewage outlets	Population discharging from outlet	Type of treatment	Discharge point relative to LWM (Low Water Mark)	Remarks	Track record
⌢⌢	**Little Perhaver** SX013417	2	2,600	Raw	At LWM	Sandy, safe swimming. Improvements by 1995 to provide full treatment and an extension to the existing sea outfall.	☐☐☐☐☐ ✓✓✓
⌢	**Portmellon** SX016439					Sand/shingle. Although this beach fulfils the requirements for a Guideline pass of the EC Bathing Water Directive it has failed the Mandatory Standard at some stage over the season and so cannot be recommended.	✓✓✓✓✓✓✓✓
f	Mevagissey SX016439	1	3,000	Raw	East of harbour at LWM	Fishing harbour. Improvement to provide interception and transfer for full treatment planned for 1995.	
⌢⌢	**Polstreath** SX017454					Intermittent problems due to Mevagissey outfall - to be resolved by 1995.	✓✓✓✓✓✓✓
⌢⌢ ⌢⌢	**Pentewan** SX018467					Sandy. Upstream sewage treatment works at Mevagissey to receive uprating, tertiary treatment and disinfection by 1994.	✗✗✗✗✓✓✓✓
⌢⌢ ⌢⌢	**Porthpean** SX032507					Small sandy bay. Designated swimming area with restricted boat launching from Spring Bank Holiday to mid September.	✓✓✓✓✓✓✓
⌢⌢ ⌢⌢	**Charlestown** SX042516					Sandy. Outfall was closed and diverted to Par summer 1993.	
⌢⌢	**Duporth** **Crinnis Beach (Par)**						☐☐☐☐ ✗✓✓✓
⌢⌢	**Golf Links** SX063522						✓✓✓✓✓✓✓✓
⌢⌢ ⌢⌢	**Leisure Centre** SX056521					Sandy. Swimming dangerous near stream. Well-managed beach.	☐☐☐☐☐ ✓✓✓
⌢	**Par Sands** SX083533						✗✓✓✓✓✓✓✓
	Spit Beach	1	21,000	Secondary	1,000m below LWM	Sandy. Dominated by china clay factory. Improvement scheme under construction, due for completion in summer 1994.	
⌢	**Polkerris** SX092521	1	60	Raw	Pumped discharge 5m below LWM	Sandy. Interim fine screening planned and then treatment to meet UWWTD standards by 2005.	✓✗✓✓✓✓✓✓
	Polridmouth Beach					Sandy beach with shelter from south-westerly winds. Water quality not monitored by NRA in 1993.	
f	**Readymoney Cove (Fowey)** SX118511	50	2,500	Raw	Generally at LWM	Sandy. Improved scheme to provide secondary treatment under construction, due for completion in 1995.	✗✗✓✓✓✗✓✗

Rating	Resort	Sewage outlets	Population discharging from outlet	Type of treatment	Discharge point relative to LWM (Low Watter Mark)	Remarks	Track record
	Lantic Bay					Sand/shingle. Strong undertow. Coastal land owned by the National Trust – further information available from them.	
	Lansallos Bay					Sand. Safe bathing. Water quality not monitored by NRA in 1993.	
f	Polperro SX210509	1	3,500	Maceration	At LWM	Pebbles.	
f	**East Looe** SX257532					Sandy.	✓✓✓✗✓✓✗
⌒⌒	**Millendreath** SX268541					Sandy.	☐✓✓✗✓✓✓✓
⌒⌒	**Seaton Beach** SX268541	1	1,300	Raw	At LWM	Grey sand and pebbles. New sewage treatment works and resewerage with transfer of flows from Downderry planned for 1995.	✗✗✗✓✓✓✗✓
⌒⌒	**Downderry** SX314538	1	1,000	Raw	At LWM east of village beach	Silvery sand. Transfer to Seaton for treatment planned for 1995.	☐✗✓✓✓✓✓✓
⌒⌒	**Portwrinkle, Freathy (Whitsand Bay)** SX359538	1	800	Macerated.	Pumped discharge at LWM	5km stretch of sand backed by cliffs. Bathing unsafe. Good access to beach via metal staircase. Improvements planned to construct a pumping station and treatment works for 1995.	☐✗✓✓✓✓✓✓
	Cawsand Bay	2		Raw	At LWM	Pebbles and rocks. Improvement scheme to intercept and transfer flows to new inland works by 1995. Water quality not monitored by the NRA in 1993.	
	Kingsands Bay	2	157 & 665	Raw	5m and 12m below	Sand and shingle. Water quality not monitored by NRA in 1993. Improvement scheme to intercept and transfer flows to new inland works by 1995.	
	SOUTH DEVON **Plymouth Hoe**						
f	**East** SX478537	Many	100,000	Primary and raw.	From LWM to 50 below LWM.	Improvements planned to give staged outfall closures from 1993 to 1998, flow transfer to new secondary sewage treatment works in central Plymouth area and existing secondary treatment sewage works.	✗✗✗✓✗✗✗✗
f	**West** SX475537						
f	**Bovisand Bay** SX493505					Sand and rocks. Polluted by untreated sewage from Plymouth outfalls.	✓✓✓✓✓✓✗
f	**Wembury** SX516485	1	4,400	Secondary	100 below	Silvery sand and rocks. Discharge point remote from beach.	✓✗✓✓✓✓✓✗
⌒⌒	**Mothecombe** SX610473					Sandy. Bathing safe only on incoming tide.	✓✓✓✓✓✓✓

14. CHALLABOROUGH, DEVON

OS ref: SX6424

Challaborough is a sheltered horseshoe-shaped cove with fine sand and rocks. At low tide there are extensive rockpools to explore and the beach is great for building sandcastles. Dogs are banned from the beach from 1 May until 30 September.

Water quality

Litter
The beach is cleaned five times a week by hand and twice a week by tractor.

Access
Take the B3392 off the A379 from Kingsbridge to Plymouth. The beach is off a minor road beyond Ringmore. Access to the beach is from the car park.

Parking
There is parking adjacent to the beach.

Public transport
The beach is not easily reached by public transport.

Toilets
There are toilets in the car park.

Food
Fish and chips and bar meals are available nearby.

see p.48

Seaside activities
Swimming, surfing and walking.

Wet weather alternatives
There is a sports and leisure club next to the beach.

Walks and wildlife
The beach is on the South-West Way. This stretch of the walk starts at Wonwell Beach on the eastern side of the River Erme estuary.

Track record

✓ ✗ ✓ ✓ ✓ ✓ ✓

15. BIGBURY-ON-SEA, DEVON

OS ref: SX6544

Bigbury-on-Sea is a pretty village with a sandy beach at the mouth of the South Devon Avon. Burgh Island, just off the beach, is connected by a causeway which is passable at low tide; at high tide there is a unique sea tractor which transports passengers to and from the island. The hotel on Burgh Island is reputed to have been the inspiration for Agatha Christie's *Ten Little Indians*. Dogs are not banned from the beach but must be kept under control.

Water quality

One outfall, serving 1,286 people, discharges primary treated sewage at low water mark.

Bathing safety

Bathing is safe, except near river mouth. Lifeguards patrol between May and September.

Access

From the village and car park.

Parking

There is a car park with space for 900 cars.

Public transport

The beach is not easily reached by public transport.

Toilets

There are toilets in the village and on the island.

Food

There is a kiosk selling food and café in the village, and a pub and hotel on the island.

Seaside activities

Swimming, surfing, windsurfing, fishing and jet skiing.

Wildlife and walks

Bigbury is on the South Devon Coast Path. Between the rivers Avon and Erme, the path follows the undulating cliff-line passing Burgh Island and the beaches of Bigbury and Challaborough. It leads on through one of the most strenuous sections of the coast path: after rounding Beacon Point walking becomes easier as the path drops down to Wonwell Beach and the Erme estuary. The many wild

flowers attract numerous butterflies in the summer.

Track record

✓✓✓✓✓✓✓

➤ **For map position see p.47**

Rating	Resort	Sewage outlets	Population discharging from outlet	Type of treatment	Discharge point relative to LWM (Low Watter Mark)	Remarks	Track record
⌒⌒	**Bigbury-on-Sea, South** SX651441	1	1,260	Secondary	50m below	Sandy. Swimming dangerous near river mouth. Popular with windsurfers.	✓✓✓✓✓✓✓✓
⌒	**Bantham** **Thurlestone**					Sand and mud. Bathing dangerous.	✓✓✓✓✓✓✓✓
⌒⌒ ⌒⌒	**North** SX674421					Red sand. Sheltered swimming. Good for windsurfing.	☐☐☐✗✗✗✓✓

49

16. SOUTH MILTON SANDS, THURLESTONE, DEVON

OS ref: SX6741

South Milton Sands is owned by the National Trust and is in an Area of Outstanding Natural Beauty. The beach is comprised of coarse sand with rocky outcrops and has plenty of rock pools to explore at low tide. The most prominent feature in the area is the famous Thurlestone Rock painted by Turner, which is best seen at high tide. The name Thurleston comes from the Saxon name Torleston meaning pierced stone. Dogs are not banned from this beach.

Water quality

Bathing safety
Bathing is safe so long as you follow the advice given by lifeguards and observe the warning flags.

Litter
Cleaned regularly in the summer.

Access
Thurlestone is off the A379 on minor roads from Kingsbridge to Modbury.

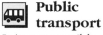

Parking

There is a car park immediately next to the beach.

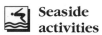

Public transport

It is not possible to get to the area of the beach using public transport.

Toilets

There are toilets at the car park.

Food

There is a café at the car park.

Seaside activities

Windsurfing, swimming, snorkelling, golf and walking. There is a windsurf school at the beach.

Wet weather alternatives

None are available at the beach.

Wildlife and walks

Thurlestone is on the South West Coast Path. South Milton Ley is the second largest reedbed in Devon and provides an important habitat for reed and sedge warblers and migrating birds.

Track record

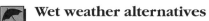

Rating	Resort	Sewage outlets	Population discharging from outlet	Type of treatment	Discharge point relative to LWM (Low Water Mark)	Remarks	Track record
⌃⌃	**Hope Cove** SX675397					Sandy. Flows transferred for treatment inland.	✓✓✓✓✓✓✓✓
	Soar Mill Cove					Stream crossed sands, rock pools and cliffs. Water quality not monitored by NRA in 1993.	
⌃⌃	**Salcombe North Sands** SX731382	4	3,400	Macerated and raw	At LWM and 50m below.	Sandy. Full treatment by 1995.	✗✓✓✗✓✗✓✓
f	**Salcombe South Sands** SX720850	1	70	Raw	7m below LWM.	Sandy. Improvements under construction to new inland sewage treatment works as for Salcombe North Sands by 1995.	✗✓✗✓✓✓✓✗

17. MILL BAY, NEAR SALCOMBE, DEVON

OS ref: SX7438

Mill Bay is a privately owned beach across the estuary from Salcombe. This fine sandy cove is sheltered and is set in a beautiful rural area with gentle slopes down to the beach. The picturesque village of East Portlemouth is about 1km (1,100 yards) away although it is a steep climb to get there by foot. This beach is very popular with visitors despite being off the beaten track. During the Second World War Mill Bay was used as an American base. Air sea rescue boats were moored in the harbour and an anti-aircraft battery was sited on the cliffs above the beach.

Water quality

Bathing safety
There is no lifeguard cover but bathing is generally safe

Litter
The beach is regularly cleaned.

Access
The easiest approach to the beach is by passenger ferry from Salcombe.

Parking
There is a car park nearby. It is easy walk from the car park to the beach.

Public transport
There are bus services to Salcombe and from there take the ferry across the estuary to Mill Bay.

Toilets
There are toilets nearby.

Food
The nearest café is about 1km (1,100 yards) away.

Seaside activities
Swimming, windsurfing and walking.

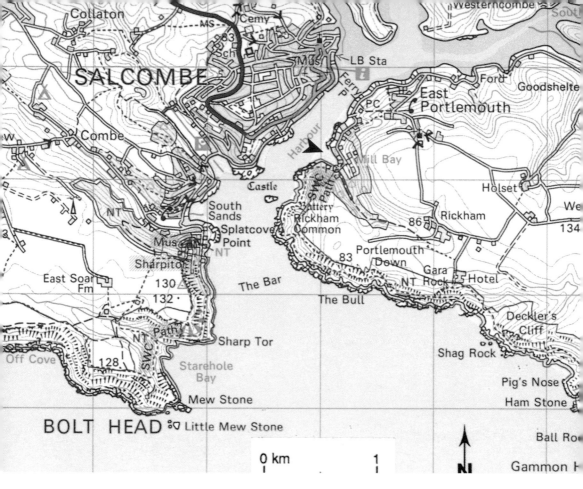

 Wet weather alternatives
There are none at the beach.

 Wildlife and walks
Walk leaflets are available from the local tourist information centres.

Track record

| ✓ | ✗ | ✓ | ✓ | ✓ | ✓ | ✓ |

Rating	Resort	Sewage outlets	Population discharging from outlet	Type of treatment	Discharge point relative to LWM (Low Watter Mark)	Remarks	Track record
	Hallsands					Shingle. Interesting ruined village nearby. Water quality not monitored by NRA in 1993.	
	Beesands					Shingle, steeply shelving. Water quality not monitored by NRA in 1993.	
⌒⌒ ⌒⌒	**Torcross** SX823419	1	300	Raw	Pumped discharge at LWM south of village	Small fishing port.	⬜⬜⬜⬜✓✓✓✓

18. SLAPTON SANDS, DEVON

OS ref: SX8445

A 4.5km (3 mile) stretch of shingle beach extending from Pilchard Cove in the north to Torcross in the south. The main road from Dartmouth to Kingsbridge runs along the edge of the beach, with a large, reed-rimmed freshwater lake (Slapton Ley) on the other side. The village of Slapton itself is about 1.5km (1 mile) inland. The beach was used in 1943-44 as a practice area for the D-day landings and all the local villages were evacuated while the US army took over the area. A Sherman tank has been salvaged from the sea and is on display in Torcross as a memorial, and opposite the lane to Slapton there is a stone obelisk put up by the US army as a 'thank you' to the local people. As can be expected on such a long, open beach, it is often very windy but the views all round Start Bay are spectacular. At low tide it is possible to walk round the headland from Torcross to Beesands, the next cove along, but if you get cut off there is an arduous walk back on the cliff path.

Water quality
There is one outfall serving 889 people discharging primary treated sewage 30m (33 yards) below low water mark.

 ## Litter
Sometimes littered, particularly after bad weather.

Bathing safety
Bathing is generally safe, but the beach shelves steeply – beware of the undertow. Sometimes large fragments of wartime debris are thrown up by the sea so be careful when swimming. There is a zoned bathing area at Torcross and a beach patrol in the summer.

Access

The A379 runs along the edge of the beach; access is easy.

Parking

There are car parks at Strete Gate, Torcross and approximately half-way down the length of the beach.

Public transport

Either take the bus from Plymouth to Slapton Sands or take the bus from Totnes to Kingsbridge and then the bus from Kingsbridge to Torcross.

Toilets

There are toilets in Torcross and at the car parks.

Food

There are shops, cafés and pubs in Torcross.

Seaside activities

Swimming, fishing, and a children's play area at Strete Gate.

Wet weather alternatives

Field Study Centre at Slapton Ley.

Wildlife and walks

The area is rich in differing habitats and the Slapton Ley Field Centre organises guided walks throughout the summer. On the edges of the beach itself the unusual Yellow Horned Poppy can be found, which should be admired, not picked. Slapton Ley itself is the largest body of fresh water in the south-west of England and as a result is a mecca for many species of wildfowl and other animals. At Torcross there is a hide (with disabled access) to allow panoramic observation across the Ley and also a corner where children can feed the ducks and swans. There is a 3km (2 mile) circular walk starting and finishing at Torcross – the South Devon Circular Walk.

Track record

✓✓✓✓✓✓✓

19. BLACKPOOL SANDS, STOKE FLEMING, DEVON

OS ref: SY8747

Blackpool Sands is a complete contrast to its Lancashire cousin. The only development of this beach, an unspoilt cove at the northern end of Start Bay, comprises a car park, a kiosk serving takeaway food and drink and a toilet block. A crescent of coarse golden sand around 1km (1,100 yards) long is flanked by steep, wooded cliffs. On the southern side of the cove below Matthew's Point a valley opens to the shore, from which a stream, Blackpool Lake, flows across the moderately shelving sands into a pool, very popular among families with small children. Easy access and safe bathing make the beach very popular. Dogs are banned from the beach between May and September.

Water quality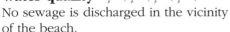

No sewage is discharged in the vicinity of the beach.

Bathing safety

Bathing is safe, but care is required as the beach shelves steeply.

Access

Blackpool Sands are signposted from Dartmouth on the A379. South of Stoke Fleming a side road leads to the car parks.

Parking

There are three car parks.

WC Toilets

There are toilets at the car park.

Food

There is a takeaway with off-licence and beach barbecue.

Seaside activities

Swimming, windsurfing, sailing, fishing and diving. Toppers, windsurf boards and canoes are available for hire. Sailing and windsurfing school with RYA instructors.

Wildlife and walks

North of the beach the South Devon Coast Path can be followed, passing through Stoke Fleming to the entrance to the Dart Estuary. South, the footpath leads to Strete Gate along the 8km (5 mile) sweep of Start Bay and on towards Start Point.

Track record

Rating	Resort	Sewage outlets	Population discharging from outlet	Type of treatment	Discharge point relative to LWM (Low Water Mark)	Remarks	Track record
	Leonard's Cove	2	1,000 1,000	Raw Raw	At LWM At LWM	Shingle. Outfalls discharge at Stoke Fleming. Water quality not monitored by NRA in 1993.	
🐦🐦	**Dartmouth Castle & Sugary Cove** SX886502	5	11,900	Raw	At LWM to 50m below	Shingle. New full treatment works, flow transfers and outfall planned for 1995.	✔✔✔✔✔✔✔✔
🐦🐦	**St Mary's Bay** SX932551	1	90,000	Raw/maceration	220m below LWM off Sharkham Point	Sand and pebbles. Improvement scheme. New full treatment works, flow transfers and outfall planned for 1998.	✔✔✔✔✔✔✔✔
🐦🐦 🐦🐦	**Shoalstone Beach** SX932566					Pebbles.	✔✔✔✔✔✔✔✔
🐦🐦	Churston Cove SX919569					Shingle.	☐☐☐☐☐☐☐✔
🐦🐦 🐦🐦	**Broadsands Beach** SX897574					Muddy sand and pebbles.	✔✔✔✔✔✔✔✔
🐦	**Goodrington Sands** SX893594					Sand and pebbles. Storm water overflow.	✔✖✔✔✔✔✔✔
🐦	**Paignton** **Paignton Sands** SX894606					Red sands. Storm water overflow.	✔✔✖✔✔✔✔✔
🐦🐦	**Preston Sands** SX896617					Red sands. Storm water overflow.	☐☐☐✔✔✔✔✔
🐦🐦	**Hollicombe** SX8988621						✔✔✔✔✔✔✔✔
🐦🐦	**Torre Abbey Sands** SX909635						✔✔✔✔✔✔✖✔
🐦🐦	**Beacon Cove** SX919630						☐✔✔✔✔✔✔✔
🐦🐦 🐦🐦	**Meadfoot Beach** SX930630					Sandy at low tide.	✔✔✔✔✔✔✔✔
🐦🐦	**Anstey's Cove/ Redgate Beach** SX930648	1	100,000	Fine screened	Pumped discharge 50m below LWM	Sand and shingle. Outfall off Hope's Nose. Flow interception and pumping to treatment works planned for 1998.	✔✔✔✔✔✔✔✔
🐦🐦	**Babbacombe** SX930654					Shingle.	✔✔✔✔✔✔✔✔

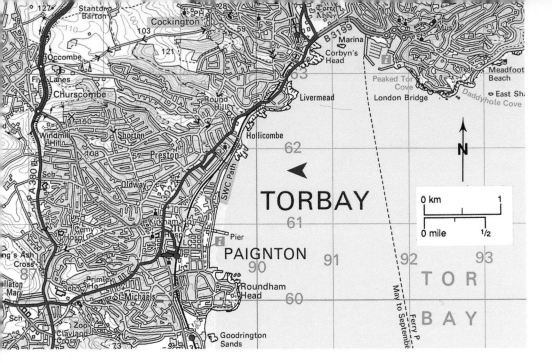

20. TORBAY, DEVON

OS ref: SX9366

Torbay is one of the most famous and popular seaside areas in Britain. Known as the English Riviera on account of the mild climate and abundant palm trees, the large bay has numerous beaches some of which have good water quality. As expected in a large holiday area there are lots of things to do locally, and trips inland. Dogs are banned from most of the beaches between May and September.

Water quality

At Oddicombe, Maidencombe and Ness Cove.

 Litter

All the major beaches are cleaned daily over the summer season.

Bathing safety

Generally bathing is safe. All beaches fly red flags when bathing is believed to be unsafe.

P ⊘ WC Parking, food and toilets

There are numerous facilities at the beaches.

Public transport

To get to Oddicombe, take the 23 or 32 bus from Torquay to St Marychurch. To get to Maidencombe, take the 85 bus from Torbay to Maidencombe. To get to Ness Cove, take the 85 bus from Teignmouth to Shaldon.

Seaside activities

There are many activities including swimming, fishing, sailing, and there are opportunities to hire boats and pedalos.

Wet weather alternatives

The English Riviera Centre in Torquay. Kent's Cavern Show Caves, Paignton Zoo, Torbay Aircraft Museum, Compton Castle, Berry Pomeroy Castle, the Dart Valley Railway and the beautiful village of Cockington are all within reach. Leaflets available from the local tourist offices.

![wildlife icon] **Wildlife and walks**

The South Devon Coast Path extends round the bay and offers some of the most glorious views on the south coast. More information is available from the local tourist offices.

Track record

Oddicombe	✓ ✓ ✓ ✓ ✓ ✓ ✓
Maidencombe	✓ ✓ ✓ ✓ ✓ ✓ ✓
Ness Cove	✓ ✓ ✓ ✓ ✓ ✓ ✓

Rating	Resort	Sewage outlets	Population discharging from outlet	Type of treatment	Discharge point relative to LWM (Low Water Mark)	Remarks	Track record
⌒⌒	**Watcombe Beach** SX926673					Sand.	✓✓✓✓✓✓✓
⌒	**Shaldon** SX935723	1	50,000	Primary and secondary	Pumped discharge 2,400m below LWM	Sandy. Improvement scheme completed summer 1993.	✗✗✗✓✓✗✓✓
⌒	**Teignmouth** SX943728					Sandy. Flows transferred summer 1993 - improvements in water quality should become apparent in 1994.	✓✗✓✓✓✓✓✓
⌒	**Holcombe** SX956746					Rocky. No sewage outfall, flows transferred summer 1993.	☐☐☐✗✓✓✓✓
	Dawlish						
⌒⌒	**Town** SX965768						✓✓✓✓✓✓✓
⌒⌒	**Coryton Cove** SX961760	1	12,000	Raw	100m below LWM	Red sand/shingle. Town beach affected by sewage-related debris. Improvements planned to provide resewerage and treatment by the year 2000 to meet the UWWTD.	☐☐☐☐☐☐✓✓
⌒⌒	**Dawlish Warren** SX983787					Sand and dunes. Bathing dangerous near river. Sewage-related debris is sometimes a problem.	✓✓✓✓✓✓✓
f	**Exmouth** SY983787	1	42,700	Primary	170m below	Sand. Strong tides. Bouyed area dedicated to wind surfing. Lifeguards Sundays and Bank Holidays. Improvements planned for 1995. Sewage-related debris a problem.	☐☐☐✓✓✓✓✗
f	**Sandy Bay** SY033798					Red sand.	✓✓✓✓✓✓✗
f	**Budleigh Salterton** SY069819	1	5,066	Raw	50m below HWM	Pebbles sloping steeply.	✓✗✓✓✓✓✓✗
⌒	**Ladram Bay** SY119895					Pebbles.	☐✓✓✓✓✓✓✓
⌒	**Sidmouth** SY127872	1	14,000	Maceration/ screens	400m below LWM pumped discharge	Pebbles/sand. Improvements planned to provide treatment by 2000 to meet the UWWTD.	☐☐☐☐☐✓✓✓
⌒⌒	**Sidmouth: Jacob's Ladder** SY119869						✓✓✓✓✓✓✓

21. BRANSCOMBE, DEVON

OS ref: SY2188

A quiet, undeveloped 5km (3 miles) of pebble beach stretching from Beer Head to Weston Mouth. A wide valley opens to the coast at Branscombe Mouth with grassland stretching down to the edge of the beach. The cliffs and crags to the east are chalk, whereas to the west there are steep red sandstone cliffs. At Weston Mouth, a stream flows down a steep grassy valley to the beach which is more secluded.

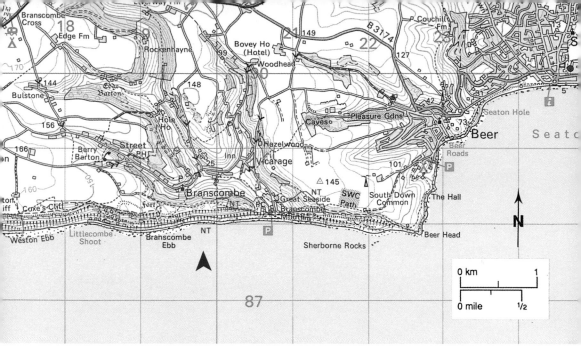

Water quality

 Litter
A clean beach which is normally free from litter.

 Bathing safety
Safe bathing.

Access
Branscombe is signposted off the A3052 between Sidmouth and Seaton. At Branscombe Mouth there is a short level walk from the car park to the beach.

P Parking
There is a car park with 400 spaces next to the beach.

WC Toilets
There are public toilets in the beach car park.

Food
There is a café on the beach.

 Seaside activities
Swimming, windsurfing, sailing, diving, and fishing. Boats are available for hire.

Wet weather alternatives
Roman camp, pottery, forge and bakery all open to the public.

Wildlife and walks
East of Branscombe, walks along the Hooken Cliffs take you to Beer Head. In the other direction the South-West Way follows the cliffs to Weston, Sidmouth and beyond. The area is geologically very interesting with landslips, deep cut valleys and fossils. There is a varied and interesting flora and the rock pools in the area abound with life.

Track record
No track record is available.

Rating	Resort	Sewage outlets	Population discharging from outlet	Type of treatment	Discharge point relative to LWM (Low Watter Mark)	Remarks	Track record
🐦🐦	**Beer** SY231891	1	2,000	Raw	At LWM 1km south of the town	Pebbles. Steep beach.	✔✔✔✔✔✔✔
🐦🐦 🐦🐦	**Seaton** SY245898					Pebbles. Steep beach. Improvement scheme.	✔✘✔✔✔✔✔✔
	DORSET						
	Lyme Regis:						
f	**Monmouth Beach** SY337915						✘✘✘✘✘✘ ✘
🐦	**Church Beach** SY343921						☐☐☐☐☐ ✘✘✘
f	**Cobb Beach** SY339918	1	6,000	Raw	15m below LWM	Sandy. Resewerage and flow transfers under construction, to new tertiary inland works - due for completion in 1995.	☐☐☐☐☐ ✔✘✘
🐦	**Charmouth West** SY636930						✘✔✔✔✔✔✔✔
f	**Charmouth East** SY367929	1	8,145		1km offshore	Sand/shingle. Flow storage, screening, pulse discharge at ebb.	☐☐☐☐☐ ✘✔✘
🐦	**Seatown** SY446910					Pebbles.	✔✔✔✔✔✔✔
🐦🐦 🐦🐦	**Eypemouth** SY446910					Shingle beach with excellent rock pools exposed at low tide. Beach surrounded by unstable cliffs of geological interest.	☐✘✔✔✔✔✔✔
🐦	**West Bay** SY459904	1	30,000	Maceration/ screens	1.5km below	Steep, shingle beach. Littering/marine debris a problem. Although this beach fulfils the requirements for a Guideline pass of the EC Bathing Water Directive it has failed the Mandatory Standard at some stage over the season and so cannot be recommended.	✔✔✔✔✔✔✔
🐦	Burton Bradstock SY490887					Shingle.	☐☐☐☐☐☐ ✔✔
🐦🐦	**Chesil Cove** SY682735	1	86,000	Maceration/ screens	1.3km below	Pebbles. Swimming very dangerous.	☐☐☐☐☐ ✔✔✔
🐦🐦 🐦🐦	**Church Ope Cove** SY6971					Sheltered cove beneath the rugged cliffs of the Isle of Portland. Shingle with boulders Unsuitable for bathing.	✔✔✔✔✔✔✔
	Portland Harbour						
f	**Sandsfoot** SY673772					Sandy.	✔✔✔✔✔✔✘✘
🐦🐦	**Castle Cove** SY676775					Sandy.	☐☐☐☐☐ ✔✔✔

Walkers in Dorset can expect spectacular views, such as this of Old Harry Rocks.

Rating	Resort	Sewage outlets	Population discharging from outlet	Type of treatment	Discharge point relative to LWM (Low Watter Mark)	Remarks	Track record
	Weymouth						
⌒⌒	South SY682789						✔✔✔
⌒⌒	**Central** SY681794					Sand/shingle and pebbles. Watersports and bathing areas segregated. Lifesaving equipment at Pleasure Pier. Dog ban from May to September. Beach cleaned daily in summer. Many facilities in the town.	✔✔✔✔✔✔✔✔
⌒⌒ ⌒⌒	Lodmoor West SY687806						✔✔✔
⌒⌒ ⌒⌒	**Lodmoor** SY688807					Long shingle beach backed by the coast road and RSPB nature reserve.	✔✔✔
⌒⌒ ⌒⌒	**Bowleaze** SY704818					Fine shingle and sand.	✔✔✔✔✔✔✔✔
f	**Ringstead Bay** SY751813					Shingle and pebbles.	✔✔✔✔✔✔✔✘

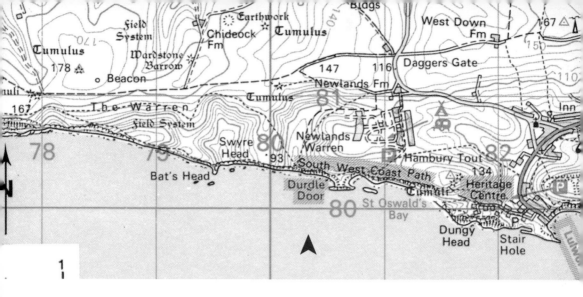

22. DURDLE DOOR, DORSET

OS ref: SY2188

This beach is famous for Durdle Door Arch, created by the great erosive power of the sea and probably the most photographed view along the Dorset coast. The eastern end of the beach (Durdle Door Cove) is protected by the arch while the rest of the beach is partially protected by a submerged offshore reef that dries in places along its length. The beach is a narrow strand of mixed shingle, gravel and sand which makes a strenuous kilometre (1,100 yard) walk to the western end where Bat's Head, a chalk headland, forms an attractive boundary to the beach itself. All the cliffs backing the beach are steep and prone to occasional rockfalls – thus climbing or sheltering underneath them is not advised.

Water quality

No sewage is discharged in the vicinity of this beach.

Litter
A small amount of marine litter, including plastic, rope and wood is washed up in Durdle Door Cove.

Bathing safety
Care is required as with most shingle and gravel beaches since there can be sudden steep slopes underwater. The western end of the beach may be cut off under certain tide and wave conditions.

Access
The beach is approached by

steep 800m (880 yard) footpath from the cliff top car park. Access on to the eastern end of the beach down a steep flight of steps cut into the bay cliff can be slippery in wet weather.

P Parking
There is a large cliff top car park at Durdle Door Caravan Camping Park (with excellent views across Weymouth Bay to the Isle of Portland).

WC Toilets
There are toilet facilities at the caravan park.

Food
There is a café and store in the caravan park.

![icon] Seaside activities

Swimming, diving, snorkelling and fishing. The steep access to the beach means that heavy equipment, including picnic tables, should not be carried down.

![icon] Wildlife and walks

The undulating cliffs form a challenging section of the Dorset Coast Path. To the east lies Lulworth Cove and the Isle of Purbeck, to the west

Whitenothe headland. However, the reward for tackling this stretch of Heritage Coast is a fine view across Weymouth Bay and to the glorious beaches below. The chalk habitat creates picturesque downland with its accompanying flora and fauna.

Track record

West ✓✓✓✓✓✓

East ✓✓✓

Rating	Resort	Sewage outlets	Population discharging from outlet	Type of treatment	Discharge point relative to LWM (Low Watter Mark)	Remarks	Track record
⚓⚓	**Lulworth Cove** SY824799	1	2,000	Raw	Below LWM	Shingle. Discharge is outside the cove. Screens planned for 1994.	✓✓✓✓✓✓✓
	Worbarrow Bay					Closed at times due to military range. Sometimes badly littered. Water quality not monitored by NRA in 1993. Sand and pebbles.	
f	**Kimmeridge Bay** SY907790					Rocky. This beach has no sand and is formed of cobbles, stone and smooth flat rocks. Be careful near the cliffs, they are unstable.	✓✓✓✓✓✓✗
	Swanage						
f	South SZ031888						✓✓✗
f	**Central** SZ032791						✓✓✓✓✓✓✗
f	North SZ031797	1	12,000	Maceration	100m below LWM	Improvement scheme due for completion in 1994 for screening and tidal storage and subsequent primary treatment. Sandy. Outfall off headland.	✓✓✗

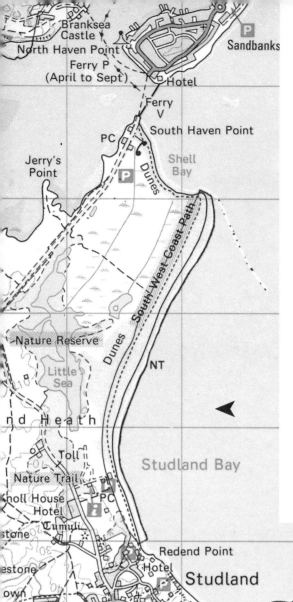

23. STUDLAND, DORSET

OS ref: SZ0483

A lovely clean beach in an Area of Outstanding Natural Beauty. 5km (3 miles) of excellent sandy beach are backed by unspoilt dunes. The beach sweeps south from the entrance to Poole Harbour to the chalk cliffs of Handfast Point, once connected to the Needles of the Isle of Wight, which are visible on the horizon most days. The beach can be divided into three areas – south beach, middle beach and the north or Knoll beach. Behind Knoll beach there is a brackish lake and marsh area which forms the Studland Heath National Nature Reserve. Visitors should note that the eastern end of the beach is used by naturists. Dogs should be kept on a lead and bylaws require that dog faeces are removed by the owners. A leaflet about Studland and the surrounding area is available from the National Trust.

Water quality

There is no sewage discharged in the vicinity of this beach.

Litter

This is very clean beach due to the excellent efforts of the National Trust.

Bathing safety

Safe bathing off the main beach; strong currents at the entrance to Poole harbour make bathing at the northern end of the beach unsafe. The beach is patrolled by National Trust wardens from Easter to September.

 ### Access
Each section of the beach is signposted from Studland village. There is a short walk from the car parks to the sands. There is a wheelchair ramp at Knoll beach.

Parking
Four car parks provide parking for 3,500 cars.

Toilets
There are five blocks of toilets. Those at middle and Knoll beach have facilities for disabled visitors and facilities for nursing mothers are at Knoll beach.

Food
There are many cafés and kiosks.

Seaside activities
Swimming, windsurfing and sailing. Windsurf boards are available for hire.

Wildlife and walks
The Studland Heath National Nature Reserve behind the beach contains a brackish lagoon, Little Sea. The reserve cannot be reached from the beach but must be entered from the road which bounds its western edge. There is a wide variety of wildlife including the rare Smooth snake and adders. Walkers are advised to wear stout shoes and to stay on the marked paths. The Dorset Coast Path starts, or alternatively, finishes, at the entrance to Poole Harbour. It follows the bay south and on to the Foreland. From the path there are splendid views of the cliffs and the chalk pillars, Old Harry and Old Harry's Wife, which are isolated from the adjacent headland by the ever-eroding waves. The path continues south towards Ballard Point with fine views of Swanage Bay.

Track record
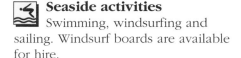

24. SHELL BAY, DORSET

OS ref: SZ0386

Shell Bay is a fine sandy beach backed by dunes. The main attraction of the beach is the shallow and warm water. The beach is very close to the Studland Heath National Nature Reserve.

Water quality

Access

The beach is approached by road from Corfe Castle and Swanage and by car ferry from Poole and Bournemouth.

Parking

There is a car park nearby.

Seaside activities

Swimming.

Wildlife and walks

The nearby Studland Heath National Nature Reserve has many dune, woodland and heathland trails with regular guided walks. There is a birdwatching hide at Little Sea.

Track record

Rating	Resort	Sewage outlets	Population discharging from outlet	Type of treatment	Discharge point relative to LWM (Low Watter Mark)	Remarks	Track record
	Poole						
⌒	**Rockley Sands** SY972908						✓✓✓✓✓✓✓
⌒⌒	**Lake** SY983904						✓✓✓✓✓✓✓✓
⌒⌒	**Harbour** SZ049885						✓✓✓✗✓✓✓✓

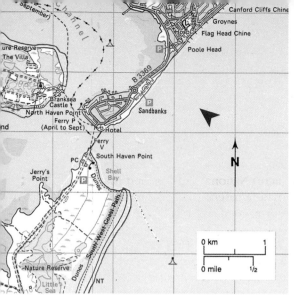

25. POOLE SANDBANKS, DORSET

OS ref: SZ0588

An extremely well-managed and popular beach with consistently good or excellent water quality. From North Haven Point at the end of the Sandbank Spit, the fringe of golden sand stretches 5km (3 miles) north-east to merge with the beaches of Bournemouth. The pedestrian promenade is backed by the steep pine- and shrub-covered Canford Cliffs. Flaghead Chine, Cranford Chine and Branksome Chine cut through the cliffs to the beach. South-west, the cliffs give way to the low-lying Sandbanks peninsula at the mouth of Poole Harbour. Here the beach is edged by dunes and overlooked by holiday development and the Sandbanks Pavilion and recreation area. The whole of Poole Harbour is a centre for sailing and water sports, and there is an ever-changing boating scene at the harbour entrance. There are excellent views across the harbour and of Brownsea Island from Evenning Hill off the western shore road. A removal of canine faeces bye-law and dog ban between Sandbanks and Branksome Chine is in force from May to September, and dogs must be kept on a lead on the promenade.

Water quality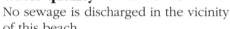

No sewage is discharged in the vicinity of this beach.

Litter
The beach is cleaned daily.

Bathing safety
Bathing is safe, except at the extreme western end of the beach near the harbour entrance. Warning signs indicate where not to swim. Segregation of bathers and powered vessels is actively encouraged, with a buoyed area in which boats must observe a strict speed limit. The beach is patrolled by lifeguards at weekends and on bank holidays from May to September, and there is a first aid post manned by St John Ambulance at weekends.

Access
There is easy access along the length of the beach; paths lead down the cliffs to the promenade. Disabled access is available to the promenade at Sandbanks, Branksome Chine and Branksome Dene Chine.

Parking
There are seven car parks along the length of the beach with 1,400 spaces. There is also parking available on adjacent streets.

Toilets
There are toilets, with facilities for disabled visitors and mother and baby rooms, along the beach.

Food

There are cafés and kiosks close to the beach.

Seaside activities

Swimming, windsurfing, sailing, and fishing. There are windsurf boards and boats for hire. Poole Harbour has several windsurfing and sailing schools. There is also a putting green, crazy golf and a variety of children's amusements.

Wet weather alternatives

Tower Park leisure complex incorporating Splashdown, Ice-Trax, Mega-Bowl, multi-screen cinema and sports centre; swimming pool, aquarium, Guildhall Museum, Archaeological Museum, Royal National Lifeboat Museum, Maritime Museum, Waterfront Museum, Arts Centre and Poole Pottery, Poole Park.

Wildlife and walks

There is a car and pedestrian ferry from North Haven Point to Shell Bay, where the Studland Heath National Nature Reserve backs an excellent beach. There is also a pedestrian ferry to Brownsea Island. Around 80 hectares (198 acres) of this 202 hectare (500 acre) National Trust-owned island is a nature reserve run by the Dorset Trust for Nature Conservation. Many types of habitat are to be found on the island including heathland, woodland, freshwater lakes, salt marsh and the seashore. There is a nature trail and guided walks are available during the summer. Further information is available from the National Trust shop on the island's landing quay.

Track record

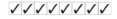

Rating	Resort	Sewage outlets	Population discharging from outlet	Type of treatment	Discharge point relative to LWM (Low Watter Mark)	Remarks	Track record
⌒	Branksome Chine SZ066897					Sand/shingle. Muddy at low tide. Although this beach fulfils the requirements for a Guideline pass of the EC Bathing Water Directive it has failed the Mandatory Standard at some stage over the season and so cannot be recommended.	✔✔✔
⌒⌒ ⌒⌒	Alum Chine SZ076903					Windsurfing popular.	✔✔
⌒⌒ ⌒⌒	**Durley Chine** SZ078903						✔
⌒⌒ ⌒⌒	**Fisherman's Walk** SZ128913						✔
	Bournemouth						
⌒	**Bournemouth Pier** SZ08890					In emergencies sewage from the inland works may be discharged at Bournemouth and Boscombe. Lifeguards in summer. Many car parks and a 10 kilometre promenade along the seafront. Dog ban from May to September.	✔✔✔✔✔✔✔
f	**Boscombe Pier** SZ112911						✔✔✘

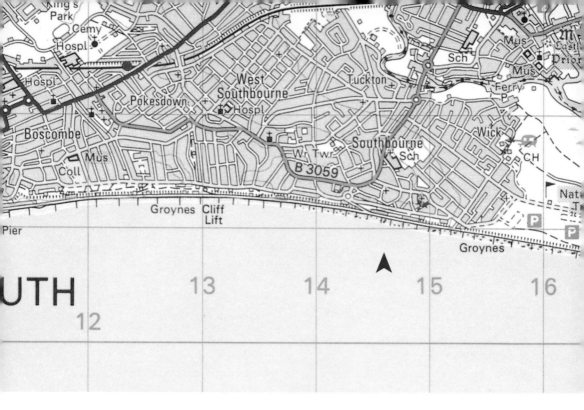

26. SOUTHBOURNE, NEAR BOURNEMOUTH

OS ref: SZ1491

Southbourne is a sandy beach with safe swimming. Its golden sands are backed by steeply sloping shrub covered cliffs. Southbourne is close to the holiday centre of Bournemouth which has all the usual attractions.

Water quality

 Bathing safety
Generally safe bathing.

 Access
Southbourne is just east of Bournemouth and is easily reached by car and public transport.

 Parking
There is plenty of parking.

WC **Toilets**
There are extensive toilet facilities along the promenade.

 Food
There are numerous catering facilities along the promenade into Bournemouth.

Seaside activities
Swimming, surfing, windsurfing, sailing and fishing. The nearby town of Bournemouth has all the main seaside attractions including museums, exhibitions, concerts and summer shows.

Track record

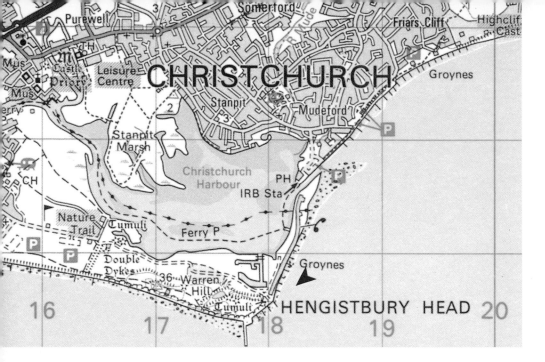

27. HENGISTBURY HEAD, CHRISTCHURCH, DORSET

OS ref: SZ1590

The 1.6km (1 mile) long Hengistbury headland separates Poole Bay and Christchurch Bay and encloses Christchurch Harbour on its landward side. Most of the headland remains undeveloped and has been designated as a Site of Special Scientific Interest because of the wide variety of plant and animal life it supports. There are two distinct beach areas. Hengistbury Head itself is a south facing pebble beach below the imposing sandstone cliffs. This 3km (2 mile) stretch of beach is undeveloped. In sharp contrast is the sand spit stretching north from the headland to the entrance of Christchurch Harbour. A string of beach huts face the groyne-ribbed sands. A ferry from Mudeford crosses the harbour entrance to drop passengers at the northern end of the beach where there is a quay and short promenade.

Water quality

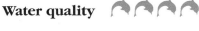

Litter
This beach is sometimes affected by marine litter from boats moored nearby.

Bathing safety
On the seaward facing side of the headland bathing is safe except near the entrance of the harbour.

Access
A land train transports visitors to Hengistbury Head and via a ferry from Mudeford.

Parking
There are 500 spaces at Hengistbury Head and 360 at Mudeford Quay.

Toilets
There are five blocks of toilets along the main beach.

Food
There is a beach café.

Seaside activities
Swimming and windsurfing. There is a windsurfing school nearby.

Wildlife and walks
Hengistbury Head is of considerable archaelogical interest with evidence of Iron Age and Roman settlement. There are information signs to interpret the history and wildlife of the area and there is a nature trail.

Track record

✓✓✓✓✓✓✓

Rating	Resort	Sewage outlets	Population discharging from outlet	Type of treatment	Discharge point relative to LWM (Low Water Mark)	Remarks	Track record
	Christchurch						
◝	**Mudeford Sandbank** SZ183912						✓✓✓✓✓✓✓✓
f	Mudeford Quay SZ183915						☐☐☐☐☐✓✗✗
◝◝	**Avon Beach** SZ183912						✓✗✗✓✓✓✓✓
◝◝	**Friars Cliff** SZ192252						☐☐☐☐☐✓✓✓
◝◝	**Highcliffe Castle** SZ200929						☐☐☐☐☐✓✓✓
◝◝	**Highcliffe** SZ216931					Sailing harbour. Shingle and mud. Rivers Avon and Stour contain treated sewage giving a high coliform bacterial count in the harbour.	✓✓✓✓✓✓✓✓
	Isle of Wight						
◝	**Totland** SZ322871	1	2,000	Maceration	300m below	Shingle. To be transferred to Norton by 1993.	✗✓✓✓✓✓✓✓
◝	**Colwell Bay** SZ328879					Shingle.	✗✓✗✓✓✓✓✓
	Yarmouth	1	1,000	Raw	170m below	Sailing harbour. Flows to be transferred to Norton by end of 1993. Shingle beach. Water quality not monitored by NRA in 1993.	
◝◝	Norton SZ347898	1	15,000	Maceration	230m below LWM	Sandy.	☐☐☐☐☐✓✓✓
◝◝	**Gurnard Bay** SZ477959	1	5,800	Maceration	400m below	Shingle.	✗✗✗✓✗✗✗✓
	Cowes						
◝◝	**West** SZ488967	1	15,000	Screens	Long sea outfall 700m below LWM.		✗✗✗✗✗✗✗✓
◝	**East** SZ506964					Sailing centre.	☐☐☐☐☐✓✓✓
	Ryde						
◝◝	West SZ588930						✗✗✗✗✓✗✗✓
◝◝	**East** SZ601927	1	21,000	Maceration	3km below LWM	Sandy.	☐☐☐☐☐✓✓✓
	Seaview					Sandy and rocks. Bathing safe. Sewage transfer to Ryde. Water quality not monitored by NRA in 1993.	
◝◝	**Bembridge** SZ657881	1	7,000	Maceration/ tidal tank	800m below	Sailing centre. New scheme planned for 1995 to give preliminary treatment and a long sea outfall.	✗✗✗✗✓✗✗✓

The Isle of Wight and Cowes in particular is famous for yachting.

Rating	Resort	Sewage outlets	Population discharging from outlet	Type of treatment	Discharge point relative to LWM (Low Watter Mark)	Remarks	Track record
↷	**Whitecliff Bay** SZ657881					Sandy.	✓✓✗✗✓✓✓✓
↷↷	Yaverland SZ610849	1	50,000	Primary	250m below	Sandy.	☐☐☐☐☐ ✓✓✓
↷↷	**Sandown Esplanade** SZ601842					Sandy.	☐☐☐☐☐ ✓✓✓
f	Shanklin SZ589827						✓✗✓✓✓✓✓✗
↷↷	**Shanklin Chine** SZ585811					Sandy.	☐☐☐☐☐ ✓✓✓
f	**Ventnor** SZ562773	2	5,300	Maceration	At LWM	Sandy. Improvement scheme to give preliminary treatment and a long sea outfall by 1995.	✗✗✗✗✓✗✗✗

28. COMPTON BAY, ISLE OF WIGHT

OS ref: SZ3841

This is a lovely rural beach owned by the National Trust in an Area of Outstanding Natural Beauty. The beach itself is made up of shingles and extends for about 1km (1,100 yards). The cliffs are a part of the Hanover Point to St Catherine's Point Site of Special Scientific Interest renowned for its geological features as wells as the fact that it supports a number of interesting plants and insects. There are superb views across the bay to Tennyson Down and in clear weather the Dorset coast at Purbeck can be seen to the west.

Water quality

No sewage is discharged in the vicinity of this beach.

Litter

The beach is cleaned regularly from Easter to the end of September and daily from the beginning of July to mid-September by the National Trust. The beach is sometimes susceptible to litter deposits after strong south westerly winds, particularly in winter.

Bathing safety

The beach is considered to be safe. Emergency telephones and lifebelts are available. There are no lifeguards but the beach is patrolled by National Trust staff from the early July to mid-September. There is an inshore rescue boat station just over 1km (1,100 yards) away at Freshwater Bay.

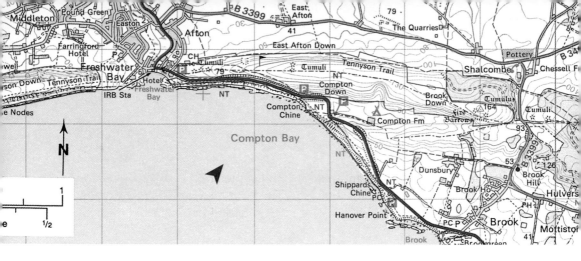

Access

The beach can be accessed from two places, however neither way is easy. Hanover car park provides the closest access to the beach but this is via a steep ramp which is sometimes destroyed by the tide in winter. The steps are rebuilt and maintained in the summer months. At the Compton Chine end of the beach the car park is situated beside the Compton Farm track. To get to the beach, cross the main road then follow a path round the edge of the field, then descend several flights of steps before reaching the beach.

P Parking

There are two car parks providing space for about 400 cars.

WC Toilets

There are toilets run by South Wight Borough Council in the Hanover car park. These are open from April to October and include facilities for disabled visitors.

Food

A van sells ice-creams and hot food at Hanover car park.

Seaside activities

Swimming and surfing.

Wildlife and walks

Compton Bay is on the Isle of Wight Coastal Path and adjoins many areas of National Trust land including the downs following on the chalk cliffs at the western end of Compton Bay. The Bay is the home of the rare Glanville Fritillary butterfly, found on the eroding cliffs. The cliff and the downs are famous for many rare and interesting species of plant and insect.

Track record

✓✓✓✓✓✓✓

Rating	Resort	Sewage outlets	Population discharging from outlet	Type of treatment	Discharge point relative to LWM (Low Water Mark)	Remarks	Track record
⌒⌒	**St Helens** SZ637892	1	1,500	Raw		Sandy.	✓✗✗✗✓✓✗✓
f	**Seagrove Bay** SZ632912					Connected to Ryde.	✓✓✗✗✗✗✗✗

Rating	Resort	Sewage outlets	Population discharging from outlet	Type of treatment	Discharge point relative to LWM (Low Watter Mark)	Remarks	Track record
	HAMPSHIRE						
⌢⌢	**Barton-on-Sea** SZ239928	1	17,400	Primary	At LWM	Pebbles and shingle. Effluent is disinfected prior to discharge. Scheme under construction to transfer flows to new treatment works at Pennington to provide secondary treatment by 1995.	☐☐☐ ✓✓✓✓
⌢	**Milford-on-Sea** SZ283915					Pebbles. Sometimes affected by marine debris. Improvements as above.	✗✗✗✗✓✓✗✓
⌢⌢ ⌢⌢	**Lepe** SZ456985					Sand and shingle.	✓✓✓✓✓✓✓✓
⌢⌢	**Calshot** SU481012					Mud. Outfall closed, no sewage is discharged in the vicinity of this beach.	✓✗✗✓✓✓✓✓
⌢⌢	Solent Breezes. SU505038						☐☐☐☐☐ ✓✓✓
⌢⌢ ⌢⌢	**Hill Head** SU548180					Good winds for experienced windsurfers, big swell when winds high.	☐☐☐☐☐ ✓✓✓

SOUTH-EAST ENGLAND

THIS CHAPTER OF *THE READER'S DIGEST GOOD BEACH GUIDE* COVERS THE AREA FROM BARTON-ON-SEA IN HAMPSHIRE TO HEACHAM IN NORFOLK. BETWEEN THESE TWO SITES LIES SOME OF THE MOST VARIED AND STUNNING COASTAL SCENERY IN BRITAIN, FOR THE SOUTH-EAST COAST OF ENGLAND IS RICH IN COASTAL CONTRASTS.

•

The scenery of the south-east coast ranges from long shingle banks to sand dunes and salt marshes. Low clay cliffs predominate in Suffolk, creeks and mud flats are found on the Essex coast and the Thames estuary. Where the chalk hills of the North Downs reach the coast the formidable white cliffs of Dover are formed. The famous white cliffs are one of the most potent symbols of Britain and form an impressive setting to many busy holiday resorts. Lowestoftness in Norfolk is the most easterly point of Britain and is continually being eroded by the North Sea. Much of the Norfolk coast is designated as an Area of Outstanding Natural Beauty and is carefully managed to promote sustainable tourism.

The Solent is busy with boating traffic and the naval base of Portsmouth is a treasure store of British maritime history housing famous ships such as the *Mary Rose*, HMS *Warrior* and HMS *Victory*. There are also ports of a very different nature – the ferry terminals of Felixstowe, Dover and Folkestone provide a gateway to Europe, the Thames estuary bears the reminders of a rich maritime past and is the site of popular boating areas such as the Medway, the Blackwater estuary and the Swale.

The South-East has some of the most heavily developed and densely populated coastal stretches, and with the people and the popularity have come problems. Heavy shipping traffic in the Channel is a continual problem with marine litter and oil constantly being washed up on to the beaches. International legislation to prevent such pollution is in place, but it is obviously being widely ignored. Extensive stretches of the coastline suffer from pollution by sewage, although action is being taken at many sites in the south. One source of pollution, sewage sludge dumping off the Thames estuary, must end by 1998, but other discharges, both nuclear and industrial, are still a cause for concern. The disturbance around Shakespeare Cliff from the construction of the Channel Tunnel will have a severe long-term effect on marine and coastal life. On a coastline under pressure from diverse human activities such as tourism, industry, and residential development, continual effort is needed to ensure improvement of the coastal environment, and to ensure that those areas which have been left unspoilt are allowed to remain so.

LEFT: The White Cliffs of Dover.

29. LEE-ON-THE-SOLENT, HAMPSHIRE

OS ref: SU5700

A long, gently curving ribbon of groyne-ribbed shingle with sand at low tide faces the Solent, with views of Southampton Water and across to the Isle of Wight. The residential development along Marine Parade overlooks this uncommercialised beach. Marine Parade West is separated from the beach by the Solent Gardens, which slope down to a promenade on two levels edging the shingle. Another promenade and flat lawns separate Marine Parade East from the beach. The steep shingle may not be the most comfortable for sunbathing on but it is popular with the more active beach user.

There is a designated area for water skiing and jet skiing, and recommended launching areas for windsurfers. There is always something to watch from the shore, whether it is the water sports or the continual shipping traffic plying the Solent. Dogs are banned from the central section of the beach from May to September inclusive. Dogs on the promenade must be kept on a lead and must not foul the footpaths or the adjoining grass verges.

Water quality

One outfall serving 200,000 people discharges secondary treated sewage 1,100m (1,200 yards) below LWM from Peel Common, to the north of Lee.

Litter

The beach is cleaned regularly by the local authority. Heavy usage of the Solent leads to problems on the beaches, with marine debris and oil being washed ashore.

Bathing safety

Safe bathing. Water skiers and jet skiers must use the areas buoyed near the Daedalus slipway and windsurf boards should be launched from the Hill Head end of the beach.

Access

Lee-on-the-Solent is signposted from the A32; the B3385 leads to Marine Parade running parallel with the shore. There is level access and ramps

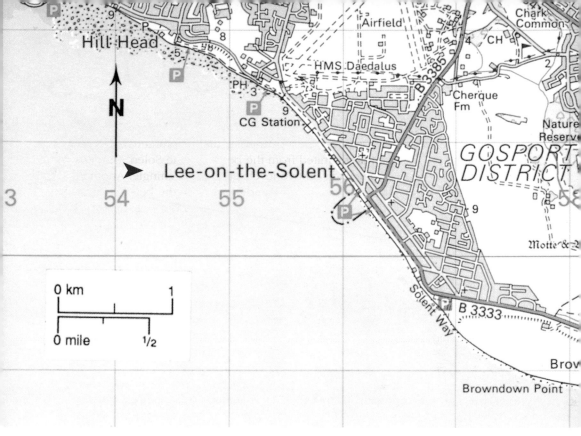

to the promenade from which there are steps and ramps to the shingle.

Parking

Two car parks with approximately 250 spaces are signposted off Marine Parade; two other car parks with approximately 150 spaces are located at the Hill Head end of the beach.

Toilets

At the Solent Gardens. Marine Parade East and Marine Parade West.

Food

There are shops and cafés on Marine Parade opposite the Solent Gardens and pubs overlooking the promenade at Hill Head.

Seaside activities

Swimming, water skiing, jet skiing, sailing and windsurfing.

Wet weather alternatives

In Gosport there is a local museum, Fort Brockhurst and a submarine museum.

Wildlife and walks

The Solent Way coastal footpath can be followed in either direction from the beach. To the north it skirts the Titchfield Haven Nature Reserve and continues along the shore to the River Hamble, an extremely popular yachting centre. To the south it can be followed to Stokes Bay. A section of the grassland adjacent to the Daedalus slipway has been set aside as a conservation area.

Track record

✓✓✓✓✓✓✓

30. STOKES BAY, GOSPORT, HAMPSHIRE

OS ref: SZ5998

The arc of Stokes Bay, with its almost manicured shingle, curves from the No2 Battery Fort south to Fort Gilkicker, fortifications built in 1860 to protect the western approaches to Portsmouth Docks. The narrow band of shingle, which shelves quite steeply to some sand at low tide, widens landward towards the south east of the bay; the long shore drift currents continually move the shingle in this direction and this has led to the build-up of a wide area of flat shingle stretching towards Fort Gilkicker. The beach, overlooking Ryde on the Isle of Wight, has a wide-open feel about it. The promenade is level with the shingle and is backed by flat grassed recreational areas which are in turn bordered by the trees and shrubs of the adjacent park and school. Popular for water sports; windsurfers can be seen throughout the year. Dogs are banned from certain areas of the beach. Dogs on the promenade must be kept on a lead and should not be allowed to foul.

Water quality
One outfall serving 200,000 people discharges secondary treated sewage 1,000m (1,100 yards) below low water mark from Peel Common, to the north of Lee-on-the-Solent.

Litter
The beach is cleaned regularly by the local authority. Heavy use of the Solent by shipping leads to problems on the beaches; marine debris is frequently washed ashore.

Bathing safety
Safe bathing. Swimming and windsurfing is restricted to specific signposted areas of the beach. There is an inshore rescue boat station at the southern end of the bay.

Access
Stokes Bay is signposted from the B3333 between Lee-on-the-Solent and Gosport. There is easy parking off the road behind the beach and level access on to the shingle.

Parking
Car parks are signposted at each end of the beach and at its centre, with over 300 spaces. There is also some parking adjacent to the promenade towards the western end.

Toilets
At the car park adjacent to the No2 Battery Fort, on the promenade near the sailing club and at Gilkicker.

Food
Café on the promenade.

Seaside activities
Swimming, windsurfing, sailing, canoeing and diving. Two public slipways. Children's paddling pool, miniature golf and tennis courts behind the beach.

Wet weather alternatives
In Gosport there is a local museum, a submarine museum and Fort Brockhurst.

Wildlife and walks
The Solent Way footpath can be followed south east past Fort Gilkicker towards Portsmouth Harbour or north-west to Lee-on-the-Solent and beyond.

Track record

✓ ✗ ✓ ✓ ✓ ✓ ✓

Rating	Resort	Sewage outlets	Population discharging from outlet	Type of treatment	Discharge point relative to LWM (Low Watter Mark)	Remarks	Track record
f	**Southsea (South Parade Pier)** SZ653982					Shingle. Improved stormwater management and further treatment being planned.	✓✗✗✓✓✓✓✗
☂☂ ☂☂	**Eastney** SZ675988	1	200,000	Screens	5km below	Shingle. New long sea outfall and improved fine screens.	✓✓✗✓✓✓✓✓
☂	**Hayling Island (East)** SZ729984					Shingle/sand. Although this beach fulfils the requirements for a Guideline pass of the EC Bathing Water Directive it has failed the Mandatory Standard at some stage over the season and so cannot be recommended.	✓✓✓✓✓✓✓✓

31. HAYLING ISLAND, WEST BEACH, HAMPSHIRE

OS ref: SZ7059

There are 8km (5 miles) of pebble beach with sand at low tide stretching along Hayling from Eastoke Point at the entrance of Chichester Harbour to Sinah Common at the entrance of Langstone Harbour. The western end of the beach is undeveloped, backed by dunes and a golf course on Sinah Common.

Water quality

Bathing safety
Bathing at either end of the beach is unsafe due to the harbour currents. Coastguard on the cliffs south of South Hayling.

Access
Reached by the A3023 from Havant. There is a short walk from the promenade across the dunes.

Parking
There is plenty of parking besides the beach.

Toilets
There are public toilets including facilities for disabled visitors.

Food
There are several kiosks and cafés.

Seaside activities
Swimming and windsurfing. Golf course.

Wet weather alternatives
Amusement arcades.

Wildlife and walks
The walk along the old railway line to the north of the town takes you along the west shore of Langstone Harbour and leads to a nature reserve covering and area of marshland.

Track record

✓✓✓✓✓✓✓

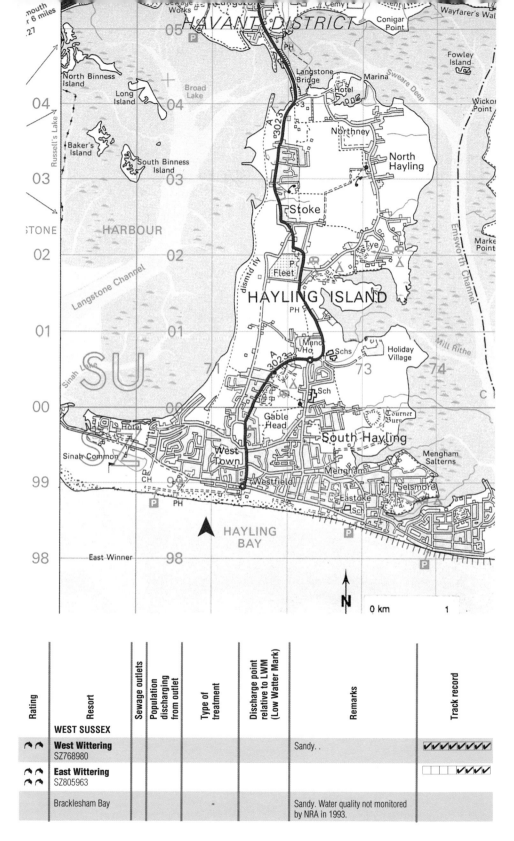

Rating	Resort	Sewage outlets	Population discharging from outlet	Type of treatment	Discharge point relative to LWM (Low Watter Mark)	Remarks	Track record
	WEST SUSSEX						
⌒⌒	**West Wittering** SZ768980					Sandy. .	✓✓✓✓✓✓✓✓
⌒⌒ ⌒⌒	**East Wittering** SZ805963						□□□□✓✓✓✓
	Bracklesham Bay		▪			Sandy. Water quality not monitored by NRA in 1993.	

32. SELSEY BILL, HAMPSHIRE

OS ref: SZ8693

From the low headland of Selsey Bill with its excellent views of the Isle of Wight, the beach extends in both directions. The groyne-ribbed east beach is the most popular, backed by the sea wall, the shingle and sand beach stretched to Pagham Harbour. The lifeboat station and the fisherman's compound add to the interest. The west beach is backed by private land and stretches away to East Wittering round Bracklesham Bay.

Water quality

Bathing safety
Fast currents around Selsey Bill make it unsafe to bathe there.

Access
There is direct access to the beach from the sea wall.

Parking
There is a car park at Selsey wit around 500 places.

Toilets
There are toilets available at Selse

Food
There are many kiosks.

Seaside activities
Surfing, windsurfing and sailing.

Wildlife and walks
Pagham Harbour to the east is a nature reserve and the Sidlesham Ferry Nature Trail follows the western edge of the harbour with a range of birds, butterflies and plants to be seen. The saltmarsh has a large number of visiting wildfowl in the winter.

Track record

✓ ✗ ✗ ✓ ✗ ✓ ✓ ✓

Rating	Resort	Sewage outlets	Population discharging from outlet	Type of treatment	Discharge point relative to LWM (Low Watter Mark)	Remarks	Track record
⌐	**Pagham** SZ892972					Shingle.	✓✓✗✓✓✓✓
⌐⌐	**Bognor Regis** SZ923985	1	71,500	Screens	3km below LWM	Sandy.	✓✓✓✓✗✗✓
⌐	Felpham (Yacht Club) SZ985993					Improvements planned to control storm water discharges for 1995.	☐☐☐☐☐✗✓✓
⌐	**Middleton-on-Sea** SZ985999					Sand and shingle.	✗✗✗✓✓✓✗✓
⌐	**Littlehampton** TQ040013	1	53,000	Maceration/ screens	2.5km below LWM	Sandy. Finer screens to be installed by mid 1993. Littering sometimes a problem.	✗✗✗✓✓✓✓✓
	Goring-by-Sea	1	45,000	Primary	At LWM	Sand/shingle. Safe bathing. Improvement scheme to transfer flows to East Worthing where flows will be given primary treatment prior to discharge via long sea outfall (4.5km). Improved storm water management for 1995. Water quality not monitored by NRA in 1993.	
	Worthing:						
f	East TQ168029						☐☐☐☐☐✓✗✗
f	**West** TQ91390210	1	80,000	Primary	160 below LWM	Shingle and sand. Improvement scheme planned as above for 1995.	✗✗✗✓✓✓✗✗
f	**Lancing** TQ183036					Shingle and sand. Improvement scheme planned as above for 1995.	✗✗✗✗✗✗✗✗
⌐⌐	Shoreham (Kingston Beach) TQ235046	~					☐☐☐☐☐✗✗✓
⌐	Shoreham By Sea Beach TQ214047					Commercial port. Improvement scheme planned by 1995 to provide primary treatment, long sea outfall and improved stormwater management.	✗☐✓✓✓✗✓
	EAST SUSSEX						
⌐	**Southwick** TQ214044	1	54,000	Screens	50 below	Shingle. Improvement scheme planned for 1995 as for Shoreham.	✗✗✗✓✗✗✓✓
⌐	**Hove** TQ288043	2			Storm water outfall	Pebbles/sand. Sewage-related debris sometimes a problem. Improved storm water management for 1995.	✗✗✗✗✗✗✗✓
	Brighton						
f	Kemp Town TQ323035						☐☐☐☐☐☐✓✗
f	**Palace Pier** TQ314038	3				All storm water overflows. See above for improvements.	✓✗✗✓✗✗✗✓✗
⌐⌐ ⌐⌐	**Saltdean** TQ381018					Rocky with some sand.	✓✓✓✓✓✓✓✓
	Portobello	1	300,000	Screens	1.8km below	New long sea outfall. Also see above. Water quality not monitored by NRA in 1993.	

Rating	Resort	Sewage outlets	Population discharging from outlet	Type of treatment	Discharge point relative to LWM (Low Water Mark)	Remarks	Track record
⌒⌒	**Newhaven** TV478989		7,500	Primary	Long sea outfall	Sandy beach within breakwater. Flows from East and West Newhaven have now been transferred to a new long sea outfall at Seaford.	✔✘✘✘✘✘✔✔
⌒⌒ ⌒⌒	**Seaford (East)** TV488982	1	21,500	Screens	Long sea outfall	Shingle beach is steep.	☐☐☐☐☐ ✔✔✔
⌒⌒	Cuckmere Haven TV520975					Pebbles. Bathing not safe at the mouth of the river.	✔✔✔✔✔✘✔✔
	Birling Gap					Steps down cliff to shingle beach. Many rock pools. Marine debris sometimes apparent. Water quality not monitored by NRA in 1993.	☐☐☐☐☐ ✔✔☐
	Eastbourne:						
⌒	East of Pier TV625998						☐☐☐☐☐ ✔✘✔
⌒⌒	**Wish Tower** TV614982	1	90,000	Maceration/screens 640 below		Shingle/sand. Improvement scheme under construction to provide screening, primary treatment and storm water management for 1995.	✔✔✔✔✔✔✔
⌒	**Pevensey Bay** TQ657037	1	9,590	Maceration/tidal tank	360 below	Shingle with sand. Flows to be transferred to Eastbourne for 1995. Beach affected by sewage-related debris.	✔✘✔✔✘✔✔✔
⌒	**Normans Bay** TQ682053					Shingle with sand at low water.	✔✔✔✔✘✔✔✔
	Cooden Beach					Shingle, sand at low tide. Improved storm water management for 1998. Water quality not monitored by NRA in 1993.	
⌒⌒	**Bexhill (Egerton Park)** TQ737068					Sand/shingle. Beware sand holes. Improved storm water management for 1998.	✔✔✔✔✔✔✔
⌒	Bulverhythe. TQ784086					Shingle. Long sea outfall.	☐☐☐☐☐ ✔✘✔
⌒⌒	St Leonards Beach TQ797087					Shingle, sand and rocks. Improved storm water management for 1995.	☐☐☐☐ ✔✔✔✔
	Hastings:						
f	**Hastings (Queens Hotel)** TQ819092	2	40,000		50 above 140 below		☐☐☐☐☐ ✘✘✘
⌒	Hastings Beach (Fairlight Glen) TQ862108					Shingle and sand and rockpools. New long sea outfall. Improved storm water management for 1998.	✔✘✘✔✔✘✔✔

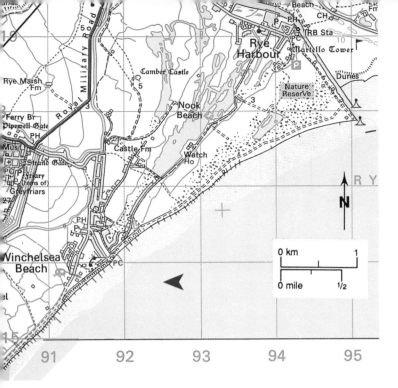

There is no sewage discharged in the vicinity of this beach.

 Bathing safety

Do not bathe when the weather is rough. There are no lifeguards.

 Access

Dogs Hill Road leads directly to the beach from Winchelsea.

 Parking

Parking is very limited.

 Public transport

There is a bus service from Rye and Hastings which stops at Dogs Hill Road, a short walk from the beach.

 Toilets

Toilet facilities are available and are cleaned daily.

 Food

There is no food available.

Seaside activities

There is a small amusement arcade in Winchelsea.

Wildlife and walks

The Rye Harbour Nature Reserve is nearby and the Saxon Shore Way.

33. WINCHELSEA, SUSSEX

OS ref: TQ9171

Winchelsea Beach is close to the historic towns of Rye and Winchelsea. It is a long ridge of pebble and shingle held in place by a sea wall and groynes. At low tide sand, rockpools and mussel beds are revealed as well as an unusual seven thousand year-old petrified forest to the east. The sea wall has a path running along the top which provides an interesting cycle ride around the edge of the nearby Rye Harbour Nature Reserve, famous for its plants, birds and insects. Winchelsea village itself is a strange, unplanned mixture of caravans, beach shacks, converted railway carriages and 1920s and 1930s architecture. Dogs are banned between May and September.

Track record

✓✓✓✓✓✓✓

Rating	Resort	Sewage outlets	Population discharging from outlet	Type of treatment	Discharge point relative to LWM (Low Water Mark)	Remarks	Track record
⌒⌒	**Camber Sands** TQ973184					Sand dunes. Ridges in sand can be a danger.	✓✗✓✓✓✗✓✓
	Broomhill Sands	1	9,500	Secondary	300m above	Sandy and coarse shingle. Water quality not monitored by NRA in 1993.	
	KENT						
⌒⌒	Greatstone Beach TR082229					Dog ban in force over the summer.	✓✗✓
⌒⌒	**Littlestone-on-Sea** TR084239	1	5,170	Secondary and UV disinfection	At LWM	Sandy.	✗✗✗✗✓✗✓✓
⌒⌒	**St Mary's Bay** TR093277					Sandy.	✗✗✗✓✓✗✗✓
⌒⌒	Dymchurch Hythe Road TR128319						✓✓✓
⌒⌒	**Dymchurch Beach** TR113304	1	6,900	Secondary and UV disinfection	Between HWM & LWM	Shingle and sand.	✗✗✗✗✓✗✓✓
⌒⌒	Dymchurch Redoubt TR101290					Pebbles and sand.	
⌒⌒	**Hythe** TR160340	1		Fine screening	2.4km below	Shingle and sand.	✗✗✗✓✗✓✓✓
⌒⌒	**Sandgate Beach** TR188348						✗✗✗✓✓✓✗✓
f	Sandgate Town Centre TR203351					Shingle. Improvement scheme planned to give primary treatment, fine screening, long sea outfall and storm water management by 1997.	✓✗✗
⌒	**Folkestone** TR237363	1	Screens	At HWM		Shingle. Improvement scheme as above.	✗✗✗✗✗✗✗✓
⌒⌒	The Warren TR248376	1	20,000	Raw	584m below	An area of conservation interest, local nature reserve, clearly marked walks giving spectacular views. Danger from falling rocks. Improvements as above. Reports of sewage-related debris.	
	Shakespeare Cliff	1	30,000	Maceration	635m below	Sand and shingle. Start of the tunnel. Water quality not monitored by NRA in 1993.	
⌒⌒	Dover Harbour TR321412					Windsurfing popular.	✓✓✓

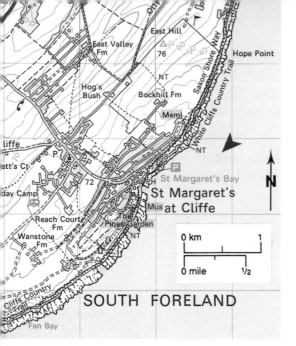

SOUTH FORELAND

34. ST MARGARET'S BAY, KENT

OS ref: TR3644

A picturesque little cove once home for both Noel Coward and Ian Fleming. The cove is sheltered by towering cliffs which form part of the white cliffs of Dover. A narrow lane leads past terraces of holiday homes to the promenade which backs the shingle, kept in place by iron groynes. The cove has been the starting point for many cross-Channel swims. There is a dog free zone on the beach.

Water quality
There is no sewage discharged in the vicinity of this beach.

Litter
There is sometimes a problem with sewage-related debris.

Access
St Margaret's at Cliffe is signposted from the A258. From the village a narrow road twists to the sea but it easier to park on the cliff top and walk down the hill.

Parking

There is a large car park behind the sea wall.

Toilets

There are toilets available.

Food

Kiosks and pubs.

Seaside activities

Swimming and diving.

Wildlife and walks

The cove is on the Saxon Shore Way with cliff top walks to Dover and Kingsdown. Access is sometimes restricted as there is a military firing range in the area. There are good views from the cliff top where the rolling heathland is owned by the National Trust.

Track record

✗✓✓✓✓✓✓

Rating	Resort	Sewage outlets	Population discharging from outlet	Type of treatment	Discharge point relative to LWM (Low Watter Mark)	Remarks	Track record
f	**Deal Castle** TR378527	3	34,480	Fine screens/ maceration tank	731m below	Steep shingle. Improvement scheme to divert flows and provide secondary treatment and improved storm water management for 1995. Path for wheelchair users. Further details of the route available from Dover District Council, Council Offices, Honeywood Road, Whitfield, Dover, Kent. ME14 2LX.	✗✗✗✗✗✗✓✗
f	**Sandwich Bay** TR358540					Sandy. Improvement scheme as above.	✗✗✗✗✗✗✗✗
↗	Ramsgate Sands TR387649						✓✓✓
f	**Ramsgate Beach** TR372640	3	20,000	Fine screens/ maceration	150m below	Sandy. Improvement scheme to provide new treatment due for 1995. Sewage-related debris reported. Dog ban.	✓✗✗✗✗✗✗✗
↗↗	Broadstairs TR401688						✓✓✓
f	**Broadstairs Beach** TR372640	1	24,160	Fine screens	3.6km	Sandy. Sewage-related debris a problem.	✗✗✗✓✗✗✓✗
↗↗	**Joss Bay** TR399702					Sandy. Poop scoop area.	✗✗✓✓✓✓✓✓
↗↗	Botany Bay TR391712					Sandy. Poop scoop area. New long sea outfall.	✓✓✓
↗↗	Palm Bay TR373714	1	56,700	Screens	1.9km	Sandy. Poop scoop area. Watersports.	✓✓✓
↗↗	Wulpole Bay TR365715					Sand, rocks. Dog ban.	✗✓
↗↗	**Margate (The Bay)** TR347708						✓✓✓✓✓✗✓✓

35. MARGATE, (FULLSOME ROCK), KENT

OS ref: TR3571

Margate has a long history as a popular seaside resort; it was here that the first covered bathing machine was first used in the eighteenth century and it remains a traditional resort with lots to do on and off the beach. The main sands at Margate stretch west from the harbour and there is an amusement arcade and funfair along Marine Terrace.

Water quality

Litter
The beach is cleaned daily by the local authority. There have been problems with sewage-related debris in the past.

Bathing safety
Lifeguards patrol the beach in summer. Bathing is safe.

Access
There are a series of steps and ramps to the beach.

Parking
Several pay and display car parks are within easy reach of the beach.

Toilets
There are toilets on the promenade with facilities for disabled visitors.

Food
There is a wide range of cafés, restaurants and eating houses within easy reach of the beach.

Seaside activities
Swimming and windsurfing.

Wet weather alternatives
Aquarium, show caves, local history museum, and life boat house. The Tourist Information Centre has information on walks and trails.

Track record
Not available.

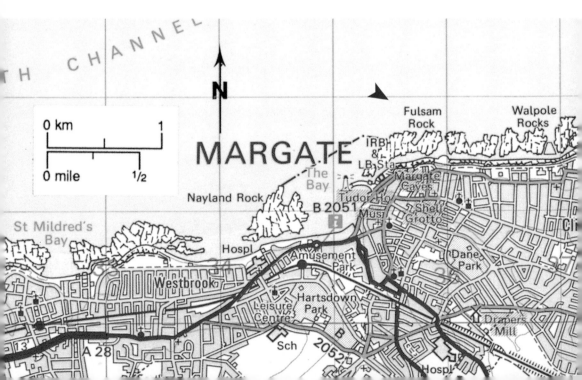

Rating	Resort	Sewage outlets	Population discharging from outlet	Type of treatment	Discharge point relative to LWM (Low Water Mark)	Remarks	Track record
⌒⌒	Westbrook Bay TR320705					Sandy. Poop scoop area.	⬜⬜⬜⬜✔✔✔
⌒⌒ ⌒⌒	**St Mildred's Bay** TR328705					Sandy. Poop scoop area.	✔✘✔✔✔✔✔✔
⌒⌒	Westgate Bay TR320702					Sandy.	⬜⬜⬜⬜✔✔✔
⌒⌒	**Minnis Bay** TR286697			Fine screens		Sand/rocks. Poop scoop area. Windsurfing popular.	✔✔✔✔✔✔✔✔
⌒	**Herne Bay** TR186686	1	10,000	Fine screens	460m below	Pebbles and sand. Improvement scheme planned for 1995 to divert flows to inland treatment works for secondary treatment prior to discharge and improved storm water management.	✔✘✘✘✘✘✘✔

36. WHITSTABLE, KENT

OS ref: TR1166

This is a quiet resort that retains much of its traditional seafaring atmosphere around the harbour and in the old town with its narrow streets, alleyways and weather-boarded cottages. Whitstable was famous for its oysters which are still produced and celebrated annually with an oyster week in July. There is also a carnival in August. Whitstable's main beach lies to the east of the harbour. Undulating grassy slopes lead gently down from Marine Parade to the promenade and sea wall which edge the pebble beach. A long bank of shingle known as the Street extends seawards from the west end of the beach. 1km (0.6m) of the bank is exposed at low water and is a good spot for collecting shells (make sure they are dead shells), but it is dangerous to swim from. From the slopes at Tankerton there are good views east along the curving beach to Swalescliffe and Herne Bay, with excellent sunsets. Swalecliffe at the eastern end of Tankerton Slopes is used by water skiers as a launching area. The sport is very popular in the Bay.

Water quality
There is one sewage outfall in the area discharging screened and macerated sewage 1,500m (1,600 yards) from the beach.

Bathing safety
Bathing is safe except near the Street where there are unpredictable currents. There are warning notices indicating where it is unsafe and a mobile coastguard lookout.

Access
Steps and ramps from the promenade.

Parking
Car parking on Marine Parade and in Gorrel Tank car park opposite the harbour.

Toilets
There are toilets at Priest and Sow Corner (near the sailing club), Beach Walk at the end of Tankerton Slopes, the harbour and Island Wall.

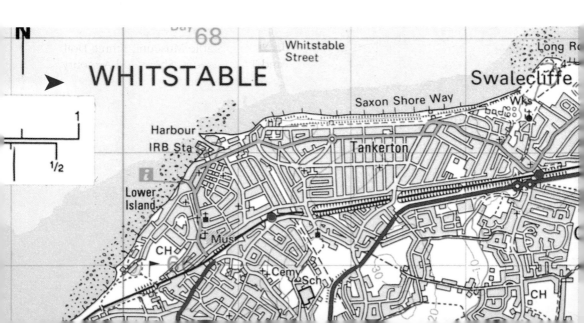

Food

There is a wide variety of cafés, restaurants, ice cream kiosks and snack bars in the town within easy reach of the beach.

Seaside activities

Swimming, windsurfing, sailing and water skiing. There are also bowling greens, tennis courts and golf courses nearby.

Wet weather alternatives

Whitstable Museum, Ethnic Doll and Toy Museum, Sherwood Armoury Museum, sports centre and bowling.

Track record

✓✓✓✓✓✓✓

The Medway estuary is as full of history as the Thames and is an important area for birds.

Rating	Resort	Sewage outlets	Population discharging from outlet	Type of treatment	Discharge point relative to LWM (Low Water Mark)	Remarks	Track record
⌃⌃	**Leysdown-on-Sea** TR025717					Sand, shingle and mud. New seawall has incorporated access for disabled visitors. Beach cleaned over the summer.	✗✗✓✗✓✓✓✓
⌃⌃ ⌃⌃	Minster Leas TQ953739					Beach cleaned over the summer.	
⌃⌃ ⌃⌃	**Sheerness** TR925750					Beach cleaned over the summer.	✓✓✓
	ESSEX						
⌃⌃	Canvey Island TQ805824	1	44,500	Secondary	At LWM	Muddy sand.	✓✓✓
⌃	Leigh-on-Sea TQ841856					Small sandy beach.	✓✓✓
⌃⌃	**Westcliff-on-Sea** TQ864853					Sandy. Improvement scheme under construction due for completion in 1998.	✗✗✗✓✓✗✓✓
⌃	Southend-on-Sea TQ887850	1	198,000	Primary	500m below LWM	Sand, shingle and mud. Improvements as above.	✓✓✓✓✓
⌃	**Thorpe Bay** TQ911847					Improvements as above.	✗✗✗✓✓✓✓✓
⌃⌃	**Shoeburyness East** TQ945852						✓✓✓
⌃⌃	Shoeburyness TQ925841					Sand and shingle. Improvements as above.	✓✓✓
f	**West Mersea** TM022120						✗✓✗
⌃⌃ ⌃⌃	**Brightlingsea** TM076161	1	9,000	Secondary	To the colne	Muddy sand. Bathing dangerous. Improvements planned.	✓✗✓✓✓✓✓✓

Felixstowe has become one of the busiest ports in Europe.

Rating	Resort	Sewage outlets	Population discharging from outlet	Type of treatment	Discharge point relative to LWM (Low Watter Mark)	Remarks	Track record
⌒⌒	**Jaywick** TM148128	1	24,000	Maceration	650m below	Sandy.	✓✓✓✓✓✓✓
⌒⌒	Clacton (off Coastguard Station) TM173142						☐☐☐☐☐ ✓✓✓
⌒⌒	Clacton (Groyne 41) TM175144						☐☐☐☐☐ ✗✓✓
⌒⌒	**Clacton (opposite Connaught Gardens)** TM187152	2			300m below 50m below	Sandy. Stormwater outfalls only. Improvements planned for 1997.	✓✗✓✓✓✓✓
⌒	**Holland-on-Sea** TM224176	1	50,000	Maceration	750m below	Sandy.	✓✗✓✓✓✓✓
⌒⌒	**Frinton-on-Sea** TM237194	2			50m below	Sandy. Storm overflows only. Treatment planned for 1998.	✓✓✓✓✓✓✓
⌒	**Walton-on-the-Naze** TM255215	1	25,000	Secondary	50m below	Sandy. See above.	✓✗✓✓✓✓✓
⌒	**Dovercourt** TM251306	1	15,000	Primary	At LWM	Sandy. Treatment planned for 1997.	✓✗✗✓✓✓✓
⌒⌒	Harwich (Sailing Club) TM263326						☐☐☐☐☐ ✓✓✓
	SUFFOLK **Felixstowe:**						
⌒⌒	**South Beach** TM297337						✗✓✓✓✓✓✓
⌒⌒ ⌒⌒	**North Beach** TM305343	2	8,400 27,000	Maceration	630m below	Red shingle and sand. Another outlet to docks serving 30,000. Improvement scheme for both beaches.	✓✓✓✓✓✓✓

37. ALDEBURGH, SUFFOLK

OS ref: TM4757

The long strip of unspoilt shingle beach falls within the Suffolk Coast and Heath Area of Outstanding Natural Beauty and the Suffolk Heritage Coast. A wide seawall protects the charming town from the continual attack of the North Sea. Colour-washed houses and hotels face this 'working' beach from which a considerable number of boats fish, selling most of their catch of crabs, lobster and a variety of fish from seafront huts. The local lifeboat is now housed in a new lifeboat station that has a viewing gallery. The beach has steep shingle ridges with some sand at low tide and stretches 3km (2 miles) north to Thorpeness. This Edwardian holiday village built around a man-made lake, The Meare, is a mixture of traditional weather-boarding combined with mock-Tudor elegance. The working windmill standing on the heathland behind the beach is also the Heritage Coast Visitors' Centre, and it is well worth a visit to find out more about this curious village and adjacent stretch of unspoilt coast.

Water quality

There is one sewage outfall serving 4,000 people which discharges macerated sewage 1,300m (1,400 yards) below low water mark.

Litter

The beach is generally clean, but subject to occasional spotting with tar and oil from passing ships. It is cleaned daily throughout the summer, but in winter littering can be considerable. Dogs are banned from May to September.

Bathing safety

The beach shelves quite steeply but evenly except at Thorpeness, where some ridges and pits in the seabed can be dangerous. It is dangerous to swim near the groynes. Lifesaving equipment is available.

Access

Level access from the road on to the promenade and across the shingle to the north.

 Parking
Car parks at each end of town adjacent to the beach. Car parks in Thorpeness can be busy on summer weekends.

 Public transport
The nearest station is at Saxmundham.

 Toilets
Public toilets at the Moot Hall, Slaugden Quay and by the coastguard station at the southern end of the promenade.

 Food
Several cafés, pubs and hotels overlook the beach. Ice-cream vendors on the promenade. Tea shop and inn at Thorpeness.

 Seaside activities
Swimming, sailing and fishing.

Wet weather alternatives
Moot Hall Museum, Thorpeness Windmill, Heritage Coast Visitors' Centre. Snape Maltings concert hall on the banks of the River Alde, a short distance inland, is the home of the Aldeburgh Festival. Gallery, craft centre, shops and restaurants at the Maltings.

 Wildlife and walks
A good map from the Tourist Information Centre details the network of paths that cover Aldeburgh and surrounding area. Aldeburgh lies on the Suffolk Coastal Path which runs from Felixstowe to Lowestoft. From the village of Snape the route follows the River Alde and joins the Sailors' Path. This crosses Snape Warren and the marshes north of the town to reach Aldeburgh beach, where shingle plants such as Sea holly and the Sea pea abound. The path continues north along the beach to Thorpeness and beyond. The Meare at Thorpeness is backed by a heathland and reedbed nature reserve managed by the Royal Society for the Protection of Birds.

Track record

38. DUNWICH, SAXMUNDHAM, SUFFOLK

OS ref: TM4770

This stretch of pebble beach forms part of a long coastal strip that is continually under attack from the waves. Dunwich village, for example, was once a sizeable town but it is now progressively falling into the sea. Between Dunwich village and Minsmere, the RSPB reserve to the south, the shingle ridged beach is backed by low sand cliffs and heathland owned by the National Trust. The heather and heath plants that thrive on the cliffs provide an attractive splash of colour when in full bloom. The steep banks of shingle which give way to sand at low tide curve northwards, protecting the low-lying meadows behind. Great care is needed to ensure that these coastal defences remain undamaged. This is a beach which is frequented more for wildlife interest rather than for any holiday beach atmosphere.

Water quality
There is no sewage discharged in the vicinity of this beach.

Litter
Some flotsam is washed up on this beach.

Bathing safety
There are war remains between low and high tide and can be dangerous for swimmers.

Access
The beach car park is signposted from the village; there is direct access on to the shingle from the car park.

Parking
There is a public car park adjacent to the beach, plus National Trust and Royal Society for the Protection of Birds (RSPB) car parks at Dunwich Heath and Minsmere.

Public transport
The nearest station is at Saxmundham.

Toilets
There are toilets in the public car park, and at Dunwich Heath and Minsmere.

Food
There is a café at the car park.

Seaside activities
Swimming and windsurfing.

Wet weather alternatives
There is a museum of local history in Dunwich. Two bird watching hides on the edge of Minsmere Reserve are open to the public free of charge; others require permits. The Coastguard cottages at Dunwich Heath have an exhibition along with a shop, tea room and toilets.

Track record

Rating	Resort	Sewage outlets	Population discharging from outlet	Type of treatment	Discharge point relative to LWM (Low Watter Mark)	Remarks	Track record
	Southwold (The Flats)	1	9,000	Secondary		Water quality not monitored by NRA in 1993.	

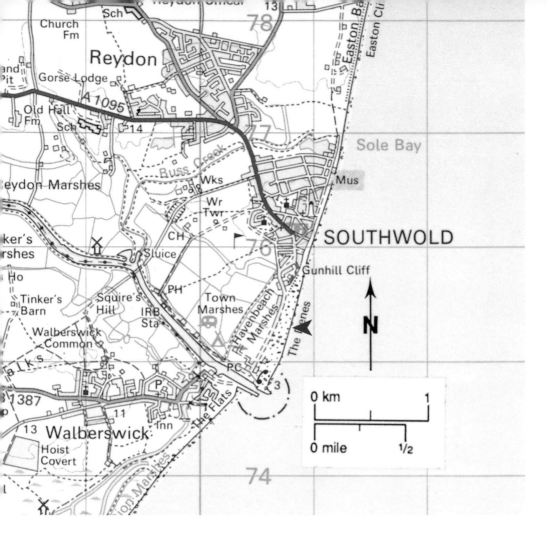

39. SOUTHWOLD, (THE DENES), SUFFOLK

OS ref: TM5076

Southwold once had a pier but all that remains is a short skeleton and the buildings on the promenade. Nevertheless, it is still the focal point for this 5km (3 mile) long beach of sand and shingle. To the north rainbow-coloured beach huts line the sea wall which edges the groyne-ribbed beach of soft sand. The beach curves northwards below sand cliffs rising to replace the sea wall. South of the pier the groyne-ribbed beach of sand and shingle stretches to the harbour at the mouth of the River Blyth. Wheeled changing huts line the promenade below scrub-covered slopes. The attractive town of Southwold sits aloft, built around seven greens and shadowed by its lighthouse.

Water quality

There is one outfall discharging secondary treated sewage.

Bathing safety

Safe bathing except near the groynes and at the river mouth. Life-saving equipment provided. The

District Council now provides a Lifeguard Service for this beach during the bathing season.

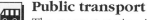 Access

The seafront is signposted within the town; car parks adjacent to the promenade/sea wall. There are steps and a steep ramp on to the beach.

P Parking

Three car parks with a total of 300 spaces adjacent to the pier and harbour.

Public transport

The nearest station is Halesworth.

WC Toilets

On the promenade, including facilities for disabled visitors.

Food

There is a café, bar, shop and takeaway at the pier.

Seaside activities

Swimming, surfing, windsurfing, sailing and fishing. Amusement arcade. Boating lake.

Wet weather alternatives

St Edmund's Hall and museum.

Wildlife and walks

There are walks along the river and across the meadows. The climb to the summit of Gun Hill is well worth the effort for the reward of some good views. The Suffolk Coastal Path runs north towards Lowestoft and south to Dunwich Forest and Minsmere, approximately 5km (3 miles) from Southwold.

Track record

					✓	✓	✓

Rating	Resort	Sewage outlets	Population discharging from outlet	Type of treatment	Discharge point relative to LWM (Low Water Mark)	Remarks	Track record
⌒⌒ ⌒⌒	Kessingland TM536867	1	5,000	Secondary		Discharges to estuary mouth 2km south of beach.	✓✓
	Lowestoft:						
⌒⌒	South Beach TM545917						✓✓✓✓✓✓✓
⌒⌒	North Beach TM554947	2	140,000	Secondary	1km below	5km of sandy beach in a busy resort with many attractions. Improvements to the outfall are planned.	✗✓✓✓✓✓✓
f	**Gorleston Beach** TG532031						✗✓✗
	NORFOLK						
	Great Yarmouth:						
f	Power Station						✗✗✗
f	**Opposite Nelson Gardens** TG533064						
f	**Opposite Marine Leisure Centre** TG533007						
⌒⌒	**Coastguard lookout** TG535010	many	75,000 including discharge to river	Fine screening	1,050m below	Sandy. Macerated sewage is discharged into the River Yare. Improvements to transfer all flows to outfall underway.	✓✓✓
⌒⌒	**Caister Point** TG530120	1	97,000		1,050m below		✓✓✓
⌒⌒	**Hemsby** TG509174						✓✓✓
⌒⌒	Sea Palling TG249412					Long sandy beach. Dog ban in force. Beach cleaned daily over the summer.	✓✓
	Happisburgh					Sandy. Water quality not monitored by NRA in 1993.	
⌒	**Mundesley** TG317366	1	7,000	Secondary/other	1,420m below	Sandy. Dog ban in force.	✓✓✓✓✓✓✓
f	Overstrand TG249412					Sand and shingle. Dog ban in force.	✓✓✗
⌒	**Cromer** TG219042	1	9,000	Tidal tank	100m below	Sandy. Dog ban in force. Improvement scheme underway.	✓✗✗✗✓✓✓
	East Runton	1	5,500	Maceration	At LWM	Sandy. Improvement scheme underway. Water quality not monitored by NRA in 1993.	
	West Runton	1	5,500	Maceration	At LWM	Sand and pebbles. Dog ban in force. Improvement scheme underway. Water quality not monitored by NRA. in 1993.	
⌒⌒ ⌒⌒	**Sheringham** TG162436	1	14,800	Maceration	260m below LWM	Sand and shingle. Dog ban in force. Improvement scheme underway.	✗✗✗✗✓✓✓

Rating	Resort	Sewage outlets	Population discharging from outlet	Type of treatment	Discharge point relative to LWM (Low Watter Mark)	Remarks	Track record
⌃⌃	**Wells-next-the-Sea** TF914456	1	7,200	Secondary	To inland drain	Sandy. Improvement scheme underway.	✗✗✓✓✓✓✓✓
	Hunstanton:						
⌃⌃	North Beach Sailing Club TF672412						☐☐☐☐☐✓✓✓
⌃	Boat Ramp TF667400						✓✓✗✓✓✓✓✓
⌃⌃	South Beach Hunstanton Road TF660395	1				Sand, stones and shingle. Storm overflow only. Sewage to Heacham treatment works.	☐☐☐☐☐✓✓✓

The Minsmere Reserve is one of the few places in Britain where the Avocet breeds.

40. HUNSTANTON, NORFOLK

OS ref: TF6742

Hunstanton is famous for its striped red and white cliffs (chalk and carrstone) and for its sunsets — it's the only east coast resort that faces west! Hunstanton is a small, friendly and well-kept resort with attractive Edwardian gardens overlooking the sea. The sandy beach is 1.5km (1 mile) long and is protected by a dog ban. Though it is a popular resort it is large enough to accommodate many visitors. For those who want a slightly quieter time of it there is an alternative in the adjoining village of Old Hunstanton.

Water quality

🧹 Litter
The beach is cleaned daily and there is adequate provision of litter bins.

◉ Bathing safety
Safe bathing except when there are off shore winds (warning flags are hoisted). Regular patrols by beach officers. Lifesaving equipment and first aid equipment available.

↗ Access
Access is direct from the promenade. There are access ramps for wheelchair users. A path for wheelchair users runs all along the promenade and round the town.

P Parking
There are five car parks close to the beach providing around 3,800 spaces.

WC Toilets
There are four sets of toilets cleaned daily, facilities are available for disabled users. Showers.

Food
Many cafés and pubs along the promenade and in the town.

Seaside activities
Swimming, windsurfing, sailing, fishing, water skiing, Punch and Judy, trampolines, funfair, organised for children, crazy golf, bowls, tennis and croquet.

☂ Wet weather alternatives
All year entertainment at the Princess Theatre; tropical pools and

giant aquaslide at the Oasis Leisure Centre, the Seal Hospital and North Sea fish at Kingdom of the Sea, and new soft play facilities at the Jungle Wonderland. Nearby is the Queen's house at Sandringham (open to the public).

Wildlife and walks

Hunstanton is at the beginning of the Norfolk Coast Path and adjoins the Area of Outstanding Natural Beauty and the Heritage Coast. There are Nature Reserves at Snettisham, Holme and Titchwell. This is an area renowned for bird watching.

Track record

Rating	Resort	Sewage outlets	Population discharging from outlet	Type of treatment	Discharge point relative to LWM (Low Watter Mark)	Remarks	Track record
↰↱	**Heacham North Beach** TF663375						✓✓✓
↰↱	South Beach TF659362						✓✓✓
↰↱	South Beach (near River) TF661368	1	32,000	Secondary/ tertiary	To river	Gravel. New treatment works completed 1990.	✗✓✓
↰↱	Snettisham Beach TF647335					Near RSPB Reserve.	✓✓✓

THE EAST COAST

THE EAST COAST SECTION OF THE *GUIDE* STRETCHES FROM THE WASH UP TO THE
BORDERLANDS OF NORTHUMBERLAND AND ENCOMPASSES SHARP CONTRASTS ALONG ITS LENGTH.
WORDS AND PHRASES SUCH AS FABULOUS, SPECTACULAR, DRAMATIC, REMOTE, WILD AND
MYSTERIOUS HAVE ALL BEEN USED TO DESCRIBE THIS AREA.
UNFORTUNATELY, LESS COMPLIMENTARY TERMS HAVE ALSO BEEN USED IN CONNECTION WITH
THIS COASTLINE – POLLUTED, SPOILT, INDUSTRIALISED AND SCARRED. INDUSTRY COMES TO THE
SHORE WITH STEEL WORKS, POWER STATIONS, OIL AND CHEMICAL WORKS, BRINGING WITH IT
DISCHARGES OF TOXIC CHEMICALS, POLLUTING THE COAST AND DAMAGING WILDLIFE.

•

Millions of tonnes of dredged spoil, sewage sludge and fly ash are dumped offshore
each year and add to the problem, although the dumping of fly ash and sewage
sludge is due to end in 1998. Waste from coal mines blackens the deserted beaches of
Tyne and Wear, Durham and Cleveland. The closure of the mines along the East coast
may lead to an improvement in the state of the beaches but ironically this may be to the
detriment of groundwater which could become contaminated by leachates from the mines.
Raw and partially treated sewage pollutes and contaminates many of the bathing waters.
Shellfish gathered from the Wash are required to be cleansed and steam cooked before
sale as the area is significantly affected by inputs of sewage. Few of the beaches in the
region escape the problem of marine litter.

However, the region still has much to offer. There are many beautiful beaches on the
East Coast and some of the most dramatic cliff walks in the country. The empty
borderlands of the north are notable for rugged cliffs, and the offshore islands were for
many years outposts for the early Christian faith. The many ruined castles of the area attest
to years of conflict between the Scots and the English. Further south, beyond the
industrialisation of the Tyne estuary, are important limestone cliffs and strange rock
formations giving way to sweeping sandy beaches and the quaint fishing villages of Robin
Hood's Bay and Filey. The Humber Estuary has huge sweeps of saltmarshes, and seals can
often be seen basking off Gibraltar Point at the margins of the Wash. The Wash is one of
the most important areas of mudflats, sandbanks and saltmarsh in the United Kingdom,
and is recognised as being of international importance as a wetland. Each year the Wash
supports over 200,000 resident and migrating birds. In the past large areas were lost to the
land for agriculture but no reclamation has been carried out since the late 1970s.

BELOW: A seal basking in the Wash.

Rating	Resort	Sewage outlets	Population discharging from outlet	Type of treatment	Discharge point relative to LWM (Low Watter Mark)	Remarks	Track record
LINCOLNSHIRE							
⌢⌢	**Skegness** TF572634					Sandy. The beach is cleaned daily. Do not bathe when the red flag is flying. Part of the Lindsey Coast improvement scheme.	✓✓✓✓✓✓✓
⌢⌢	**Ingoldmells** TF574685	1	116,000	Maceration/ screens	1,420m below	This is a privately owned beach. Public are allowed access. Sandy. Part of the Lindsey Coast improvement scheme.	✓✗✓✗✓✓✓
⌢⌢	**Chapel St Leonards** TF564722					Steeply shelving sandy beach backed by concrete promenade. Lifeguard cover at the weekends only. Part of the Lindsey Coast improvement scheme.	✓✗✓✓✓✓✓
⌢⌢	**Anderby Beach** TF553762					Sandy. Part of the Lindsey Coast improvement scheme.	✓✓✓✓✓✓✓
⌢⌢	**Moggs Eye (Huttoft)** TF550776					Gently sloping sand and shingle beach backed by dunes. Part of the Lindsey Coast improvement scheme.	✓✓✓✓✓✓✓
⌢⌢	**Sutton-on-Sea** TF522821					Sandy. Do not bathe when the red flag is flying.	✗✗✗✓✓✓✓
⌢⌢	**Mablethorpe** TF508854	1	28,000	Secondary	To inland drain	Gently sloping sandy beach backed by promenade. Lifeguard cover from Whitsun to September.	✓✗✓✗✓✓✓
HUMBERSIDE							
f	**Cleethorpes** TA310086	1	63,000	Maceration/ screens	At LWM	Sewage-related debris a problem. Improvements planned in 1995 to give secondary treatment.	✗✗✗✗✗✗✗
⌢⌢	**Withernsea** TA344281	1	12,000	Primary	940m below	Sand and shingle. Lifeguards on central promenade.	✗✗✓✓✗✓✓
⌢⌢	**Tunstall** TA322312					Sand and pebbles. Improvement scheme as above.	✓✓✓✓✓✓✓
⌢⌢	**Hornsea** TA210478	2	16,000	Screens/ maceration	1km below	Sandy with some shingle. Lifeguard cover at the weekend.	✓✓✓✓✓✓✓
⌢⌢	**Skipsea Sands** TA177572					Sandy.	✓✓✓✓✗✓✓
⌢⌢	**Barmston** TA172594					Sand and shingle.	✓✓✓✓✓✓✓
⌢⌢	**Earls Dyke** TA170615					Sandy.	✓✓✓✓✓✓✓
⌢⌢ ⌢⌢	**Fraisthorpe** TA171629					Sandy.	✓✓✓✓✓✓✓
⌢⌢	**Willsthorpe** TA172640					Sandy.	✓✓✓✓✓✓✓
⌢	**Bridlington South** TA181661	1	56,000	Screens	1.6km below	Sandy.	✓✓✓✓✓✓✓
⌢⌢	**Bridlington North** TA190672	2			At LWM	Sandy. Storm water overflows.	✓✓✓✓✓✓✓

Rating	Resort	Sewage outlets	Population discharging from outlet	Type of treatment	Discharge point relative to LWM (Low Watter Mark)	Remarks	Track record
⌒	Flamborough South Landing TA231692	1	2,176	Primary	1km below	Although this beach fulfils the requirements for a Guideline pass of the EC Bathing Water Directive it has failed the Mandatory Standard at sometime over the season and so cannot be recommended.	✗✓✗✗✗✗✗✓
⌒⌒	Flamborough North Landing TA238722					Sandy. Bathing dangerous.	✓✓✓✓✓✗✓✓
	Thornwick Bay	1	300	Primary	At LWM	Rocky. Bathing very dangerous. Water quality not monitored in 1993.	
	YORKSHIRE						
⌒⌒	**Reighton Sands** TA144763					Sand and boulders.	✓✓✓✓✓✓✓✓
⌒⌒	Filey TA120806	2	13,800	Maceration	200m below	Red sand. 1 storm water overflow.	✓✓✓✓✓✓✓✓
f	**Cayton Bay** TA067845					Sandy. Beware of incoming tide.	✓✓✓✓✓✓✓✗
	Scarborough						
⌒	**South Beach** TA046886					Sandy.	✗✗✓✓✗✓✓✓
⌒⌒	**North Beach** TA037900	1	105,000	Screened	1.5km long sea outfall	Sandy.	✓✗✓✗✓✓✓✓
⌒⌒	Marine Drive						☐☐☐☐☐☐✓✓
⌒⌒	**Robin Hood's Bay** NZ959045	1	5,500			Rocky. Swimming dangerous. Improvement scheme to be completed 1994.	✓✓✓✓✓✓✓✓
⌒⌒	**Whitby** NZ897117	1	20,000	Raw	At LWM	Sandy	✓✓✓✓✓✓✓✓
⌒⌒	**Sandsend** NZ864126	1	450	Raw	At LWM	Sand and shingle.	✓✓✓✓✓✓✓✓
⌒	**Runswick Bay** NZ811159	1	480	Raw	At LWM	Sand and shingle.	✓✓✓✓✓✓✓✓
⌒	**Staithes** NZ787190	1	4,000	Raw	At LWM	Sand and rocks.	☐✓✓✗✗✗✗✓
	CLEVELAND						
f	Skinningrove	1	9,000	Raw	At LWM	Sandy.	☐☐☐☐☐✗✓✗
f	**Saltburn-by-Sea (Pier)** NZ660217						✗✗✗✓✓✓✗✗
f	Saltburn Gill	2	13,850 6,800	Raw Raw	At LWM At LWM	Sand/pebbles. Sewage-related debris a problem Improvements planned to give full treatment by the year 2000.	☐☐☐☐☐✗✗✗
f	Skelton Beck (Beach)						☐☐☐☐☐✗✗✗
f	Skelton Beck (Footbridge)						☐☐☐☐☐✗✗✗

Rating	Resort	Sewage outlets	Population discharging from outlet	Type of treatment	Discharge point relative to LWM (Low Watter Mark)	Remarks	Track record
↶	**Marske-by-the-Sea** NZ639229	2		Storm water outfalls.	At LWM 25m below	Sandy. Sewage related debris a problem	✗✔✔
↶↶	**Redcar (Stray)** NZ625238	1	78,000	Raw	1.6km below		✗✔✔
↶	**Redcar (Granville)** NZ613251						✗✔✗✔
↶	**Redcar (Lifeboat station)** NZ606255	1		Storm water outfall Screened.	At LWM	Sand and rocks.	✗✔✔
↶↶	**Redcar (Coatham Sands)** NZ592257	2		Storm water outfall	At LWM	Sandy.	✔✔✔
↶	**Seaton Carew North Gare** NZ540286						✗✗✔
f	**Seaton Carew Centre** NZ531296	1	60,000	Storm water outfall Raw	300m below 3.5km below		✗✗✗✗✗✗✗
↶	**Seaton Carew North** NZ525305					Sandy.	✗✗✔
	Hartlepool, North Sands	3	30,000 4,300 3,600	Macerated Raw Raw	30m below At LWM At LWM	Sandy. All flows to be diverted under the terms of the UWWTD. Water quality not monitored by NRA in 1993.	
	DURHAM						
f	**Crimdon Park** NZ485373						✗✗✗ ✗✗✗✗
f	Crimdon South	1		Storm water outfall		Sandy. Improvements to divert flows due for completion in 1994.	✗✗✗
	Blackhall	1		Storm water outfall	At LWM	Sand and pebbles. Water quality not monitored by NRA in 1993.	
	Lime Kiln	1	2,500	Raw		Water quality not monitored by NRA in 1993.	✔✗
	Denemouth South	1	33,000	Screened/ tidal tank	At LWM	Sand with stones and coal waste. Improvements planned to meet the UWWTD. Water quality not monitored by NRA in 1993.	✗✗
	Horden	2	6,900 1,500	Raw Raw	Above LWM Above LWM	Sand with coal waste. Water quality not monitored by NRA in 1993.	
↶	Easington	1	8,300	Raw	50m below	Sand with coal waste. Badly polluted coastline. Improvements planned to meet the UWWTD.	
f	Dalton Burn						✗✗✗
f	**Seaham Remand Home** NZ424508	4	36,600	Raw	25m below	Improvement scheme to reduce storm water outfall use and to provide primary treatment in 1995, secondary treatment by 2000. Badly polluted coastline.	✗✗✗

Rating	Resort	Sewage outlets	Population discharging from outlet	Type of treatment	Discharge point relative to LWM (Low Watter Mark)	Remarks	Track record
f	**Seaham Beach** NZ424508	1		Storm sewage outfall	25m below	Sand.Improvement scheme due to be completed in 1995.	✗✗✗✗✗✗✓✗
f	Featherbed Rocks					Rocky area adjacent to mouth of Dalton Beck.	□□□□□□✗✓✗
	TYNE AND WEAR **The City of Sunderland**						
f	Ryhope South	2		Raw	At LWM	Sandy. Storm sewage overflows only.	□□□□□✗✗✗
f	Hendon South					Sewage debris a problem.	□□□□□✗✗✗
	Sunderland	2	500 175,000	Tidal tank Screened	At LWM 300m below	Rocky outfalls situated south of Wear Estuary. Water quality not monitored by NRA in 1993	
⌢	Roker / Whitburn South					Sandy beach with small pebbles. Lifeguard cover May to September. Beach cleaned daily.	✓✗✗✗✓✓✓✓
f	Roker / Blockhouse	1		Raw	25m below	Within the Wear estuary.Sand.Storm sewage overflows subject to extension.and screening in 1994.	□□□□□✗✗✗
f	**Whitburn** NZ407605	1		Storm sewage outfall	At LWM	Sand.	□□✓✗✗✗✗
f	**Marsden Bay** NZ400650	1		Raw and storm water outfall		Sand. Discharge from public toilet, no residential population.	✓✗✗✓✓✓✓✗
f	**South Shields (Sandhaven)** NZ379674						✗✗✓✓✗✓✓✓
f	South Shields (Inner Harbour)	2		Raw	At LWM	Within the Tyne estuary. Sand. Storm sewage overflows only.	□□□□□✗✗✗
⌢	**Tynemouth (King Edward's Bay)**. NZ373696	1		Storm water outfall	At LWM	Sand.	□□□□□✓✓✓
⌢	**Tynemouth (Long Sands South)** NZ369702					Although this beach fulfils the equirements for a Guideline pass of the EC Bathing Water Directive it has failed the Mandatory standard at sometime over the season and so cannot be recommended.	□□□□□✓✓✓
⌢	**Tynemouth (Long Sands North)** NZ366708	1		Storm water outfall	At LWM	Sand. Storm water overflow only.	□□□□□✗✗✗
⌢ ⌢	**Tynemouth (Cullercoats)** NZ365713					Sand. Lifeguard May and September. Beach maintained well and cleaned regularly. Storm water outfall.	□□□✗✓✓✗✓
⌢ ⌢	**Whitley Bay** NZ353734	10		Raw	At LWM	Long sandy beach with rocky shoals. There is a dog ban in force at the southern end of the beach. Storm water outfall only. Improvement scheme to extend outfalls being considered for 1995.	✓✓✗✗✓✓✓✓

Not only does St Abbs offer beautiful scenery, it also offers some of the best scuba diving in the country.

Rating	Resort	Sewage outlets	Population discharging from outlet	Type of treatment	Discharge point relative to LWM (Low Watter Mark)	Remarks	Track record
f	**Seaton Sluice** NZ334771	1	43,000	Tidal tank	60m below	Sandy. Improvement scheme to divert sewage for 1994. Storm water to be screened prior to discharge via existing outfall.	✗✓✗✗✓✗✗✗
	NORTHUMBERLAND						
f	**Blyth: South Beach** NZ322795					Sandy.	□□✓✓✓✓✗✗
f	Cambois South	1	26,000	Raw	50m below	Improvements planned to meet the UWWTD	□□□□□✗✗✗
f	Cambois North						□□□□□✗✗✗
⌒⌒ ⌒⌒	**Newbiggin South** NZ311873						✗✗✗✗✗✗✗✓
⌒	**Newbiggin North** NZ313878	2	29,000 5,000	Maceration Raw	At LWM At LWM	Sand. Improvement scheme to remove all discharges from the vicinity of the beach was completed in 1993. Further improvements are planned.	□□□□□✗✗✓
	Cresswell	1	200 (winter), 1,800 summer)		At LWM	Sandy. Water quality not monitored NRA in 1993.	
⌒⌒	**Druridge Bay** NZ279964					Sandy.	✓✓✓✓✓✓✓✓
⌒⌒	**Amble (Links)** NU276044~		8,000	Screens/ maceration	250m below	Rocky.	□□□□✓✓✓✓

41. WARKWORTH, NORTHUMBERLAND

OS ref: NU2606

B etween Warkworth Harbour at the mouth of the Coquet Estuary and the Aln Estuary there lies 5km (3 miles) of fabulous sandy beach. The beach, edged by sand dunes, extends northwards for 3km (2 miles) to merge with Alnmouth Links. The town of Amble lies on the southern banks of the estuary and here fishing cobles may be seen in the harbour and yachts moored in the river or at the Braid Marina. Coquet Island lies 1.6km (1 mile) off shore, sheltering the harbour entrance. The island is an RSPB reserve and boat trips are available from the harbour. The views back across the estuary with the backdrop of Warkworth Castle are most impressive. The near-perfect mediaeval village of Warkworth, an idyllic spot with dramatic castle, hermitage and unique fortified bridge is set 1.6km (1 mile) inland, almost enclosed by a meander of the River Coquet. Warkworth beach is signposted from here. The picnic site by the beach has panoramic views of the Coquet Estuary. There is access to Alnmouth Links south of Bilton on the A1068 but there is very limited parking behind the dunes.

Water quality

 Litter
Some marine litter and fishing debris is washed on to the beach.

 Bathing safety
Bathing is dangerous at high tide. There is an inshore and offshore rescue boat and coastguard station at Amble.

 Access
North of Warkworth a turning off the A1068 is signposted to the beach.

 Parking
Car park at picnic site with space for 50 cars.

 Toilets
The toilets are situated in the car park.

 Food
None at the beach. There are tea rooms in the village about 1.6km (1 mile) away.

Seaside activities
Swimming, golf course (Warkworth), river and sea fishing from Amble.

 Wildlife and walks
The picnic site and surrounding area at Warkworth beach is managed by the Northumberland National Park and the National Trust owns the land to the north. A coastal path stretches 6km (4 miles) from Warkworth to Alnmouth and is described in a leaflet available locally. A walk to the south takes you through dunes to the long breakwater serving Warkworth Harbour and some interesting saltmarshes which were designated as a Site of Special Scientific Interest in 1988. Coquet Island with its prominent lighthouse is frequented by colonies of breeding seabirds – puffins, terns, Eider. These may be viewed from boat trips around the island organised by the RSPB and information can be obtained at the Amble Tourist Information Office.

Track record

✓✓✓✓✓✓✓

Rating	Resort	Sewage outlets	Population discharging from outlet	Type of treatment	Discharge point relative to LWM (Low Watter Mark)	Remarks	Track record
⌒⌒	**Alnmouth** NU253107					Sandy. Bathing very dangerous.	✓✗✓✓✓✓✓✓
	Longhoughton Steel	1	1,200 (summer) 200 (winter)	Raw	At LWM	Sandy cove. Water quality not monitored by NRA in 1993.	
	Craster	2	400	Raw and storm water outfall	30m below	Water quality not monitored by NRA in 1993.	
	Embleton Bay					Sandy. Water quality not monitored by NRA in 1993.	

119

42. LOW NEWTON, (NEWTON HAVEN), NORTHUMBERLAND

OS ref: NU2525

Newton Haven's crescent of sand lies at the northern end of Embleton Bay. Low tide exposes a wide beach which is fringed by dunes. Sheltered by a grass headland to the north and an offshore reef, the beach is popular for watersports. It is overlooked by the village of Low Newton, an attractive square of fishermen's cottages and pub now owned by the National Trust. Behind the dunes lies Newton Pool, a freshwater lagoon which is a nature reserve.

Water quality

There is no sewage discharged in the vicinity of this beach.

Litter

Some oil drums and fishing debris are washed up, particularly in winter.

Bathing safety

Bathing is safe on the incoming tide; there are undercurrents on the ebbing tide.

Access

From the car park on the approach road to Low Newton, signposted off the B1339 from High Newton. It is a short walk down to the village with direct access to the beach. A path leads along Low Newton beach to Embleton Bay.

Parking

There is a car park 300m (330 yards) from Low Newton with space for about 100 cars. Parking in the village is for residents and disabled badge holders only.

Public transport

The beach is 1km (1,100 yards) from Embleton Station.

Toilets

There are toilets adjacent to the beach.

Food

There is a pub that serves snacks, and a tea room in High Newton 1km (1,100 yards) away.

Seaside activities

Swimming, windsurfing, sailing, diving, canoeing and fishing.

Wildlife and walks

There are bird hides at

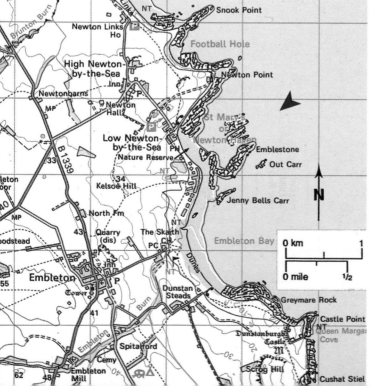

Newton Pool (one with access for disabled visitors) and a wide variety of species can be seen, particularly in winter. The Heritage Coast Path stretches south round Embleton Bay to Dunstanburgh Castle and north around Newton Point to the wide sweep of Newton Links and Beadnell Bay.

Track record

✓✓✓✓✓✓✓

Rating	Resort	Sewage outlets	Population discharging from outlet	Type of treatment	Discharge point relative to LWM (Low Water Mark)	Remarks	Track record
↷	**Beadnell Bay** NU233284					Sandy. Dangerous undercurrents at times. Although this beach fulfils the requirements for a Guideline pass of the EC Bathing Water Directive it has failed the Mandatory standard at sometime over the season and so cannot be recommended.	✓✓✓✓✓✓✓

43. BAMBURGH AND SEAHOUSES, NORTHUMBERLAND

OS ref: NU1834

A 45m (49 yard) rock outcrop towers above beautiful long sandy beaches and provides the magnificent setting for Bamburgh Castle. From the castle rock there are spectacular views of the sandy beaches stretching north to Holy Island and south to Seahouses. Seaward lies the panorama of the Farne Islands, their rocky cliffs falling steeply to the water below. It was from the Longstone Lighthouse on Outer Farne that Grace Darling set off to rescue the crew of the Forfarshire. The deed that made her a national heroine is remembered in the Grace Darling Museum in Bamburgh. Today the trip to the Islands is made from the little harbour at Seahouses. Inland, Bamburgh village nestles below the castle among undulating fields. Between Bamburgh and Seahouses there are 6.5km (4 miles) of superb beach with sand which squeaks when walked over. Backed by the St Aidan's and Shoreston Dunes, the sands give way to rocky shore at Seahouses where the rockpools are full of marine life.

Water quality

There are two outfalls at Bamburgh; one, serving approximately 1,000 people, discharges macerated sewage through a tidal tank at low water mark; the other serves 100 people and discharges untreated sewage at low water mark. One outfall at Seahouses serving 6,000 people discharges screened and macerated sewage through a tidal tank 100m (109 yards) below low water mark.

Litter

A little wood, plastic and fishing debris is washed on to the beach. Litter left by visitors is cleared by the National Trust.

Bathing safety

Bathing is safe only on the incoming tide due to undercurrents as the tide ebbs; beware of off shore winds. Life belts are available at Seahouses. There is an inshore rescue boat and lifeboat.

Access

There is access from both Bamburgh and Seahouses which lie on the B1340, with easy access to the beach across dunes.

BAMBURGH:

Parking

Large car park in Bamburgh has over 200 spaces. Three dune car parks with approximately 25 spaces in each, plus space for about 50 cars along the road above dunes.

Toilets

There are toilets available in the village.

Food

There is a café and hotel in the village, and ice-cream vans on or near the beach.

Seaside activities

Swimming, surfing, windsurfing, diving, sailing and fishing.

Wet weather alternatives

Castle, Grace Darling Museum and her grave in village.

SEAHOUSES:

Parking

Car park in village has 500 spaces. Space for 30 cars parking on verge of B1340 north of Seahouses.

Toilets

There are toilets available in the village.

Food

There is food available in the village.

Seaside activities

Swimming, golf course, amusements.

Wet weather alternatives

Marine Life Centre.

Wildlife and walks

This fantastic section of coastline falls within the Northumberland Heritage Coast and is also designated as an Area of Outstanding Natural Beauty. Below the lofty position of Bamburgh Castle, a walk north along the shore leads to Budle Bay. The salt marsh, mud and sand flats are part of the Lindisfarne Nature Reserve which covers the whole of the Fenham Flats, Holy Island Sands and most of the Island itself. The area provides feeding for thousands of waders and wildfowl. It is dangerous to cross the sands; access to the island is by the causeway which is covered for at least 11 hours each day. With its Castle and Priory, the Island is steeped in history and its distinctive conical shape leaves a lasting impression on the memory. The beaches around the island are wide and sandy but unsafe for swimming because of strong currents. The Farne Islands to the south of Holy Island are of international importance for their large colonies of seabirds and grey seals. The 30 islands that make up the Farnes are a National Trust Nature Reserve and landing is permitted on Inner Farne and Staple Island. Boats make the hour-long trip from the harbour at Seahouses in good weather.

Further information about the service is available from the National Trust shop in Seahouses. Access is restricted during the bird breeding season from mid-May until mid-July.

Track record

| Bamburgh | ✓✓✓✓✓✓✓ |
| Seahouses | ✓✓✓✓✓✓✓ |

Rating	Resort	Sewage outlets	Population discharging from outlet	Type of treatment	Discharge point relative to LWM (Low Watter Mark)	Remarks	Track record
	Holy Island	1	500 (summer) 200 (winter)	Maceration /tidal tank	At LWM	Pebbles. The best beach areas are to the east and north of the island. Water quality not monitored by NRA in 1993.	
	Cocklawburn Beach	1	15	Raw	20m above LWM north of beach	Sand and rocks. Water quality not monitored by NRA in 1993.	
↶	**Spittal** NU008515					Water quality affected by discharges in the estuary – scheme due to be completed in 1995.	✗✗✗✓✗✗✗✓
f	Spittal Quay					Affected by all discharges to the estuary. Improvement scheme.	✗✗✗
f	Berwick-upon-Tweed	1		Raw	At LWM	Sandy. Downstream of sewage treatment works	✗✗✗

CHAPTER SIX

NORTH-WEST ENGLAND AND THE ISLE OF MAN

THIS CHAPTER OF THE *GUIDE* COVERS THE NORTH-WEST COAST OF ENGLAND FROM
SKINBURNESS IN CUMBRIA DOWN TO WEST KIRBY ON THE WIRRAL AND INCLUDES
THE ISLE OF MAN.

•

The North-West Coast of England and the Isle of Man are the regions that pioneered the seaside resort and the seaside holiday. It should, therefore, be a source of national shame that there are no beaches in this area good enough to be featured in *The Reader's Digest Good Beach Guide*. There are some lovely stretches of coastline along the North-West. The huge expanse of Morecambe Bay has a panoramic view over to the Lake District. Southport, with its long beach and elegant buildings has a distinctly Victorian character and there is an extensive dune system at Ainsdale providing a habitat for rare natterjack toads and sand lizards. The National Nature Reserve in the dunes has over 10km (6 miles) of clearly marked footpaths and just to the south is Formby Point, 200 hectares (494 acres) of which is owned by the National Trust and consists of sand dunes, and pine woods.

•

The Isle of Man is a beautiful island lying in the middle of the Irish Sea – a fascinating destination often described as an island lost in time. The Isle of Man has an incredible variety of coastal scenery for such a small island with a fiercely rugged coastline contrasting with the delicate beauty of the Manx glens. Huge and gentle basking sharks are a common sight off the Isle of Man over the summer and are frequently spotted just offshore feeding on plankton. The island is easily reached by air or boat and is renowned for its hospitality, the Tourist Trophy (TT) motorcycle races and the famous Manx Kipper.

LEFT: Formby Point.

RIGHT: Bradda Head, Isle of Man.

The underlying beauty of these areas is tainted as the entire region is affected by pollution. The Irish Sea is affected by radioactive pollution and it is more chemically contaminated than the North Sea. The Mersey Estuary and Liverpool Bay have suffered particularly. It is not only accidental oil spills and pollution incidents that have caused problems but the deliberate and unacceptable discharges of mercury, cadmium and lead that are released into Liverpool Bay each day. Most of this is from industrial sources and contaminated sewage outfalls to the Mersey and its tributaries. In addition at least 1.52 million tonnes of sewage sludge and 3.56 million tonnes of dredged spoil (sediments dredged from the estuary usually contaminated with heavy metals and other persistent toxic chemicals) are dumped into Liverpool Bay each year. Some of the most famous seaside resorts in the country, such as Blackpool, look out on to this polluted sea. As a result, its beaches remain some of the most polluted in the whole of the UK.

Visitors to the beaches in the North-West must, unhappily, expect to witness pollution in some of its most distressing forms: sewage-related debris on beaches and illegally dumped refuse washed up on the shore.

Despite the plans for considerable investment in sewage treatment over the next few years, a legacy of terrible under-investment means that in 1993 there was no great improvement in the North-West's beaches. Over the 1993 bathing season the use of sodium hypochlorite as chemical disinfection was permitted on the Manchester Square outfall in Blackpool, whether this will continue over the 1994 is as yet undecided. The efficacy of chemical disinfection is in doubt and it is widely believed that it only disguises the problem of sewage pollution by removing the indicator species. It will be many years before bathing would be advisable at most beaches in this area.

The Isle of Man's beaches fare little better although industrial discharges are not as great a problem as for the mainland coast. The island does have a problem with sewage. Sewage produced in the Isle of Man is discharged to sea via short sea outfalls, most with absolutely no treatment – unsurprisingly the beaches on the island are contaminated with sewage. The EC Bathing Water Directive is not applicable to the Isle of Man but in March 1990 Tynwald, the Manx Government, decided that the EC Bathing Water Directive standards should be accepted as a target for the island. However, in 1993 only one out of eleven bathing waters tested passed the minimum legal requirements of the directive.

This situation should change drastically. The IRIS project – an ambitious scheme that aims to achieve Integrated Recycling of the Island's Sewage – will make the Isle of Man's beaches some of the best in the UK. The programme, which has the full support of the Marine Conservation Society, shows what can be done with a little imagination and is a model from which many mainland water companies should learn.

Rating	Resort	Sewage outlets	Population discharging from outlet	Type of treatment	Discharge point relative to LWM (Low Water Mark)	Remarks	Track record
⌢	**Skinburness (Silloth)** NY126565						✗✗ ✗✗✗✓
⌢⌢	**Silloth (Lees Scar)** NY094528	1	3,000	Screened	60m below	Sand and shingle. Sewage treatment works planned for 1995 providing secondary treatment and storm water management.	✗✓✗✓✗✗✓✓
f	**Allonby South** NY078424	1	300	Screened/ Tidal tank	50m below after high tide	Sand and rock slightly muddy. Popular beach. Secondary treatment works and storm water management planned for 1995. Sewage and litter reported on beach.	✗✗✗✗✗✗✗
⌢	Allonby West Winds						✗✗✗✗✓✓✗✓
	Maryport	1	11,500	Raw	Above LWM	Sand, shingle. Fishing port. Improvements planned – diversion of foul flows to proposed primary treatment works with long sea outfall at Workington for 1995. Water quality not monitored by NRA in 1993.	
	Flimby	3	100 1,500 50	Raw Raw Raw	150m above 150m above 150m above	Sand/shingle. Improvements to provide primary treatment with long sea outfall for 1995. Water quality not monitored by NRA in 1993.	
	Siddick	2	3,500 50	Raw Raw	Above LWM 200m below	Improvements planned as for Flimby. Water quality not monitored by NRA in 1993.	
	Workington	4	2,500 6,000 12,000 5,500	Raw Raw Raw Raw	At LWM 10m above 20m above Below HWM	Shingle/slag. Low amenity. Primary treatment with long sea outfall planned for 1995. Water quality not monitored by NRA in 1993.	
	Harrington	1	3,500 +industry	Raw	At LWM	Shingle/slag. Popular beach. Improvements planned as for Flimby. Water quality not monitored by NRA in 1993.	
	Parton	1	200 +industry	Screened/ maceration	800m below	Shingle/sand. Low amenity. Primary treatment planned for 1995. Water quality not monitored by NRA in 1993.	
	Whitehaven	3	500 1,000 25,500	Raw Raw Raw	Above HWM Above LWM At LWM	Shingle/black sand/cliffs. Industrial pollution. Water quality not monitored by NRA in 1993. Diversion of flows to Parton for primary treatment in 1995.	
⌢	**St Bees** NX959117	1	2,000	Primary/ tidal tank	Above LWM	Sand/shingle. Strong tank currents. Improvements planned for 1995 to include treatment and stormwater management.	✗ ✓✓✓✗✓
	Nethertown	1	500	Raw	At LWM	Sand/shingle. Water quality not monitored by NRA in 1993. Diversion of flows to primary treatment works for 1995.	
	Braystones	1	9,000	Raw	50 below	Sand/shingle. Proposed primary treatment works with long sea outfall for 1995. Water quality not monitored by NRA in 1993.	

Rating	Resort	Sewage outlets	Population discharging from outlet	Type of treatment	Discharge point relative to LWM (Low Water Mark)	Remarks	Track record
f	**Seascale** NY034010	1	2,200	Raw	Below LWM	Sand/shingle & rocks. Storm water management and a primary treatment works with long outfall proposed for 1995. Nearby radioactive discharges from Sellafield (Windscale).	✗✗✗✗✗✗✗✗
	Ravenglass	1	250 + heavy tourist trade	Primary	To Esk at LWM	Shingle and mud. Water quality not monitored by NRA in 1993.	
⌐	**Silecroft** SD120812					Sand and shingle.	✗✓✓✓✓✓✓
f	**Haverigg** SD157766					Sand dunes. High amenity. Improvement scheme including secondary treatment at Millom to ensure Haverigg compliance.	✗✗✗✗✗✗✗✗
	Millom	1	7,500	Primary	At LWM	Sand and shingle. Proposed uprating to secondary treatment for 1995. Water quality not monitored by NRA in 1993.	
f	**Askam-in-Furness** SD200788	1	2,350	Secondary To Duddon Channel		Sand. Ultra violet disinfection of secondary treated effluent planned for 1995. Askam-in-Furness and Roanhead sometimes contaminated with sheep faeces washed down from grazing mosses.	✗ ☐ ✗✗✗✗✗
	Barrow-in-Furness	32	73,000	Raw/other		All discharge to Walney Channel. Secondary treatment planned for 1996. Water quality not monitored by NRA in 1993.	
⌐⌐	**Roan Head** SD187769 **Walney Island**					Some minor littering reported.	✗✗✗✓✗✓✗✓
⌐	**West Shore** SD199857						✗✗✗✓✗✓✓✓
⌐⌐	**Biggar Bank** SD208825						✓✓✓✗✓✓✓✓
⌐	Sandy Gap SD208831					Beaches to the west of the island have sand dunes and normal bathing facilities. Walney Channel is badly polluted and used by boats only.	✓✗✓✗✓✓✓✓
f	**Newbiggin** SD314679					Sandy.	☐✗✗ ✗✗✗✗
f	**Aldingham** SD320697					Sandy.	☐✗✗ ✗✗✓✗
f	**Bardsea** SD326739					Sandy. Country park. Improvement scheme to transfer flows to Ulverston treatment works planned.	✗✗✗✓✓✗✗✗
	Grange-Over-Sands & Kents Bank	3	11,500	Secondary		Discharges to Wyke Beck. Mud, shingle and sand. New sewage treatment works. Water quality not monitored by NRA in 1993.	

Rating	Resort	Sewage outlets	Population discharging from outlet	Type of treatment	Discharge point relative to LWM (Low Water Mark)	Remarks	Track record
	Arnside	1	2,000	Tidal tank	Mud/shingle/ sand.	Water quality not monitored by NRA in 1993.	
	Hest Bank	2	2,850	Secondary	One above HWM and one below	Mud flats, sea retreats 6.5km. No bathing. Water quality not monitored by NRA in 1993.	
	Morecambe						
f	**Morecambe North** SD397658						✗ ✗✗✗✗✗✗
f	**Morecambe South** SD393653	1	31,000	Raw	At LWM	North beach mud/shingle. South beach sandy. Improvement scheme to provide storm water management and secondary treatment planned for 1996.	✗ ✗✗✗✗✗✗
*	**Heysham** SD382633					Sand. Foul flows now transferred to primary works at Lancaster which discharges to the Lune Estuary via tidal tanks.	✗✗✗✓✗✗✗✓
	Pilling Sands	1	1,000	Tidal tank	To Broadfleet	Mud flats/salt marsh. Outfall has been moved. Water quality not monitored by NRA in 1993.	
	Knott End-on-Sea					Sand/mud flats. Water quality not monitored by NRA in 1993. Flows transferred to secondary works serving Pressail then discharging to the Wyre estuary.	
f	**Fleetwood (Pier)** SD342487	1	31,000	Tidal tank	At LWM	Sand. Storm water overflow at HWM. Linked to Fylde Coast Scheme. Long sea outfall and secondary sewage treatment planned for 1996.	✗✗✗✗✗✗✗✗
f	**Cleveleys** SD312433	1	81,000			To be linked to Fylde Coast scheme for 1996. Littering by sewage and related debris a problem.	✗✗✗✗✗✗✗
f	**Bispham** SD307397						✗✗ ✗✗✗✗
	Blackpool						
	Blackpool	2	105,000	Screened	Below LWM	Sand. Discharges of storm water directly on to the beach occur once or twice a year. Improvement scheme planned. The Fylde Coast scheme – Cleveleys, Bispham and all entries under Blackpool are planned to have storm water management and secondary treatment with a long sea outfall for 1995. Planning permission has now been granted and work has commenced. This area is very badly polluted and remains highly unsuitable for bathing.	
f	**Blackpool North (Pier)** SD305364						✗✗✗✗✗✗✗✗
f	**Blackpool Lost Childrens Post** SD306356						✗✗✗✗✗✗✗✗

Rating	Resort	Sewage outlets	Population discharging from outlet	Type of treatment	Discharge point relative to LWM (Low Water Mark)	Remarks	Track record
f	**Blackpool South (Pier)** SD304338						✗✗✗✗✗✗✗✗
f	**St Anne's North** SD304305						✗✗✗✗✗✗✗✗
f	**Lytham St Anne's** SD318283	1	42,000	Screened		Sand. Beach cleaned daily. Outfall discharges to Ribble Estuary. Diversion to Preston sewage treatment works and secondary treatment by 1995.	✗✗✗✗✗✗✗✗
f	**Southport** SD322179	4	91,500	Primary	To Crossens Pool	Sandy. There are 3 storm water overflows due for closure in 1995 when treatment works extended.	✗✗✗✗✗✗✗✗
f	**Ainsdale** SD297129	0	12,000	Secondary	To inland waterway.		✗✗✗✓✓✗✓✗
f	**Formby** SD277100	0	18,000	Secondary	To River Alt	National Trust property in the area – Formby Point with Red Squirrel Reserve, leaflet available from the National Trust.	✓✓✗✓✓✗✓✗
	Hightown					Sand/mud. Emergency overflow into Alt Estuary. Water quality not monitored in 1993.	
	Blundell Sands	2	48,100			An £8 million scheme commenced in 1992 to shut these two outfalls. Water quality not monitored by NRA in 1993.	
	Brighton-le-Sands					Water quality not monitored by NRA in 1993.	
	Crosby					Water quality not monitored by NRA in 1993.	
	Waterloo					Water quality not monitored by NRA in 1993.	
	New Brighton, Victoria Road					All flows diverted to Wallasey screening plant. Water quality not monitored by NRA in 1993.	
	New Brighton, Dalmorton Road					All flows diverted to Wallasey screening plant. Water quality not monitored by NRA in 1993.	
f	**New Brighton, Harrison Drive** SJ287937					All flows now diverted to Wallasey screening plant.	✗✓✓✗✓✓✗✗
⌢⌢ ⌢⌢	**Moreton** SJ257918	1	65,000	Maceration	3km below	A long sea outfall discharges the macerated effluent through diffusers.	✓✓✓✓✓✓✓✓
	Hoylake Red Rocks					Water quality not monitored by NRA in 1993.	
	Hoylake Baths					Water quality not monitored by NRA in 1993.	

Rating	Resort	Sewage outlets	Population discharging from outlet	Type of treatment	Discharge point relative to LWM (Low Water Mark)	Remarks	Track record
f	**West Kirby** SJ210868					Sewage-related debris a problem.	✗✗
↷	**Meols** SJ230906						✓✓✗✗✗✗✗✓

THE ISLE OF MAN

Rating	Resort	Sewage outlets	Population discharging from outlet	Type of treatment	Discharge point relative to LWM (Low Water Mark)	Remarks	Track record
f	Douglas Summerhill						✓✗✓✗
f	Douglas Palace						✓✗✓✗
f	Douglas Broadway	3		Screened Raw Raw	All at LWM	The island's capital. There is a 1.6km curving beach of sand, shingle and mud.	✓✓✓✗
f	Laxey						✓✓✓✗
f	Ramsey			Raw	Below LWM	Two sandy beaches near the river mouth. Sheltered from the prevailing south westerlies. Interesting harbour town.	✗✓✗✗
f	Peel			Poorly screened	100m from shore	Sandy beach. Harbour. Peel castle.	✗✓✗✗
f	Port Erin			Raw	Tidal tank below LWM – rarely uncovered	Sandy beach in sheltered bay on south of Island. Good cliff walks nearby.	✗✓✗✗
f	Port St Mary			Raw	At LWM	Two beaches of firm, dry sand at Chapel Bay and Mary Bay.	✗✗✗✗
f	Castletown			Raw	At LWM	Domestic and industrial sewage from leather/shoe factory. Sheltered area, rocks and seaweed. Used extensively for watersports such as windsurfing.	✓✗
↷↷	Derbyhaven			Screens	At LWM – near the pier	Sheltered shingle area. Used extensively for mooring boats.	✓✓
	Gansey Bay (Bay Ny Carrickey)					Sand and shingle beach. New water sports centre. Water quality not monitored in 1993.	
f	Kirk Michael					Narrow shingle and sand beach. Exposed. Not extensively used for bathing.	✗
	Jurby	1		Raw		Narrow shingle/sand beach backed by cliffs. Exposed.	

SCOTLAND

CHAPTER SEVEN COVERS SCOTLAND, BUT EXCLUDES THE HEBRIDES, ORKNEY AND SHETLAND SINCE THE MARINE CONSERVATION SOCIETY DOES NOT HAVE ACCESS TO BATHING WATER QUALITY DATA FOR THESE AREAS. HOWEVER, IF YOU TAKE THE BOAT TO THE OUTER ISLANDS, BEACHES ABOUND AND MANY OF THEM ARE PRISTINE. THE BEACHES THAT ARE LISTED IN THIS GUIDE ARE MAINLAND BEACHES AND ARE THOSE WHICH ARE RELATIVELY EASY TO REACH FOR A DAY AT THE SEA, OR AS A STARTING POINT TO EXPLORE THE DELIGHTS OF THIS COASTLINE FURTHER. IF YOU ARE LOOKING FOR A CLEAN BEACH IN BRITAIN YOU ARE MOST LIKELY TO FIND ONE IN SCOTLAND.

•

That is not to say that Scotland does not have problems around the coast. There are Scottish beaches that have failed to meet the minimum EC bathing water quality standard. Sea-borne rubbish is washed up on to shore. Sewage sludge and dredged spoil are dumped off the Clyde, Forth and Tay estuaries. Industrial waste is discharged into coastal waters, particularly around the Clyde and the Forth. Nuclear installations at Chapelcross, Hunterston, Torness and Dounreay contribute to pollution of the sea by discharging warm water and contaminants from antifouling treatments.

Inevitably, development of the coastline has destroyed once-scenic areas. The sea lochs of the West Coast are studded with the floating cages of the troubled fish farming industry. The North Sea oil and gas industries have resulted in the growth of massive onshore terminals and the view along the Cromarty Firth is dominated by a string of platforms.

In contrast to this there is some of the most spectacular coastal scenery in the world, including the long sand dunes of the east coast, and the rocky shore of Fife with its series of picturesque fishing villages. There are also the cliffs and stacks of Caithness, and of course the West Coast, Highlands and Islands, sea lochs and towering mountains. There are hundreds (if not thousands) of beaches, tiny sandy bays, mostly remote, deserted and beautiful. Many can only be reached by the keen walker, but without a doubt the effort is well worth while.

If you are looking for peace and solitude combined with traditional hospitality then try Scotland.

LEFT: Duncansby Head.

Rating	Resort	Sewage outlets	Population discharging from outlet	Type of treatment	Discharge point relative to LWM (Low Water Mark)	Remarks	Track record
	BORDERS						
🐦🐦	Eyemouth NT945640	2	2,500 850	Raw Raw	5m above Below LWM	Rocks and sand. Bathing can be unsafe due to currents. Improvements planned for 2005 to install fine screening and primary treatment.	✓✓✓✗✓✗✗✓
🐦🐦	Coldingham Bay NT918666	1	50	Raw	12m above LWM	Sandy. Improvements to extend outfall to lowwater mark and provide septic tanks to remove gross solids.	✓✓✓✗✓✓✓✓
🐦🐦	**Pease Sands** NT794710	1	1,000	Secondary	Above LWM	Red cliffs and sand. Pease Down Woodland Nature Reserve nearby.	✓✓✓✓✓✓✓✓
	LOTHIAN						
🐦🐦 🐦	**Dunglass** NT774724					Coarse sand and rocks.	☐☐☐☐☐ ✓✓✓
🐦🐦	Thorntonloch NT753746					Mostly sandy.	✓✓✓✓✓✓✓✓
🐦🐦 🐦	Whitesands Bay NT710773					Sandy.	✓✓✓✓✓✓✓✓
f	Dunbar East NT686786					Sand and rocks. Litter clearance programme operated by local council.	☐☐☐☐☐ ✓✓✓
🐦🐦 🐦🐦	**Belhaven Beach** NT658786	1	4,200	Screens/ maceration	Long sea outfall	Sandy. Beware undertow when swimming. Litter clearance programme operated by local council.	✓✓✓✓✓✓✓✓
🐦🐦	Peffersands NT622829					Sandy. Dunes.	✓✓✓✓✓✓✓✓
🐦🐦 🐦	Seacliff NT605846					Sandy sheltered bay. Car park and toilets on private land, a fee is charged.	☐☐☐☐☐ ✓✓✓
🐦	**Milsey Bay** NT565853	2	2,100	Raw	At LWM	Sandy and rock outcrops. Litter clearance programme operated by local council.	✓✓✗✓✓✓✓✓
f	North Berwick Bay NT553855	2	2,800	Raw	At LWM	Sandy and rock outcrops. Litter clearance programme operated by local council.	✓✓✗✗✗✗✓✗
🐦🐦	**Yellowcraig (Broad Sands Bay)** NT515859	1	300	Raw	At LWM	Sandy, some rocks. Litter clearance programme operated by local council.	✓✓✓✓✗✓✗✓

44. GULLANE, EAST LOTHIAN

OS ref: NT4882

This is an absolutely beautiful and completely unspoilt 2.5km (mile and a half) sweeping sandy bay. The extensive flat sands exposed at low tide are backed by Gullane Bents, a series of 5m (16ft) high dune ridges behind which scrubland slopes up 20m (66ft) to flat grassland. Here there is parking and a picnic area, overlooked by the houses of Gullane village. The curve of sand is bounded at either end by rocky outcrops of black pillow lava. To the east there is a series of tiny sandy bays only accessible by foot along the coast path. Muirfield Golf Course overlooks this lovely bay and the view is often seen as a backdrop to televised tournaments.

Water quality

No sewage is discharged in the vicinity of this beach.

Litter
Litter is cleared daily in the summer. A litter clearance programme is operated by the local council.

Bathing safety
Bathing is safe from this beach.

Access
The beach is signposted from Gullane village on the A198 and there is a 100m (109yd) walk down through the dunes to the beach.

Parking
There is a car park with 500 places on grassland behind Gullane Bents.

Toilets
There is a toilet block at the centre of the beach.

Food
Variety of refreshments available in Gullane village.

Seaside activities
Swimming and windsurfing. There is a riding track around the bay and three golf courses. A children's play area is off the path through the dunes.

Wet weather alternatives
Golf museum adjacent to the golf shop. Luffness Castle and Myreton Motor Museum near Aberlady.

Wildlife and walks
Rock outcrops at either end of the beach contain pools rich in marine life including mussels, crabs, anemones and numerous snails. Inland the dunes are stabilised by Marram grass and the dune slacks (areas between sand ridges) have a rich and diverse population.

Track record

✓✓✓✓✓✓✓

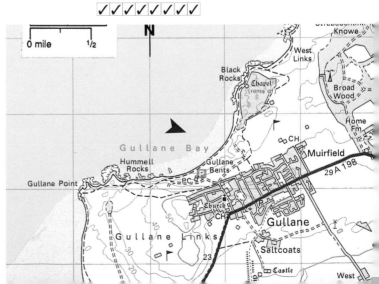

Rating	Resort	Sewage outlets	Population discharging from outlet	Type of treatment	Discharge point relative to LWM (Low Watter Mark)	Remarks	Track record
⌐⌐	Gosford Sands NT449787	1		Raw	At LWM	Sand with rocky upper shore.	✔✔✔✖✖✔✔✔
f	Longniddry NT438776	1		Secondary	At LWM	Sand and rocks. Popular with windsurfers. Litter clearance programme operated by local council.	□□□□□✔✖✖
⌐⌐	Seton Sands NT411759	1	3,700	Primary	At LWM	Sand and rocks.	✖✖✔ ✖✔✖✔
⌐⌐	Fisherrow NT323731					Sandy. Litter clearance programme operated by local council.	□□□□□✖✖✔
f	Portobello NT304745	1	4,500	Screened	At LWM	Sandy. Outfall due for removal. Remains of supports of outfall pipe from the swimming pool covered at high tide and can be dangerous.	✖✖✖✖✔✖✖✖
⌐⌐	Silverknowes NT204722					Sand and mud.	□□□□□✖✔✔
⌐⌐	Cramond NT192771					Sand, very low tide. Sewage related debris sometimes a problem.	□□□□□✔✖✔
FIFE							
	Dalgety	1	7,740	Primary	At LWM	Sand and rocks. Secondary treatment to be added after 1996. Water quality not monitored by RPB in 1993.	
⌐⌐	Aberdour Harbour NT194850	1	700	Primary	10m below	Sand and rocks. Long sea outfall to be added by 1996.	□□□□□✔✔✔
⌐⌐	**Aberdour Silversands** NT201853	1	3,300	Primary.	900m below LWM	Sandy.	✔✔✔✔✖✖✖✔
⌐⌐	Burntisland NT239858	1	20	Raw	Above LWM	Sandy. This outfall is due for diversion to treatment works in 1994-1995.	✔✔✔ ✔✔✔
⌐⌐	**Pettycur** NT264862	1	1,000	Septic tank	500m below	Sandy.	✖✖✔ ✔✖✖✔
⌐⌐	Kinghorn NT272868	1	2,400	Primary	Long sea outfall	Sandy.	✖✖✖✖✖✖✖✔
⌐⌐	**Kirkcaldy Linktown** NT281904					Sandy. The National Trust for Scotland owns several 17th Century houses in the town centre which make up Sailor's Walk.	✖✖□□✖✖✖✔
⌐⌐	**Pathhead Sands (Kirkcaldy Harbour)** NT292923	1	49,570	Fine screening	500m below	Sand/coal spoil. Improvements planned for 1996 to provide primary treatment.	□□□□□✔✔✔
f	Leven West NO386005	1	92,180	Screened	50m below	Sand/rocks. Storm water outfalls. Phased improvement scheme to include long sea outfall, primary and secondary treatment.by 2000.	□□□□□✖✖✖
⌐⌐	Leven East NO396014					Wide sands.	✔✔✔ ✖✖✖✔

Leven beach as found by the Beachwatch volunteer beach cleaners in September 1993.

Rating	Resort	Sewage outlets	Population discharging from outlet	Type of treatment	Discharge point relative to LWM (Low Watter Mark)	Remarks	Track record
⌃⌃	Lundin Links NO410022	1	1,090	Primary	200m below	Sandy to west. Rocks.	✓✓✓✓✗✓✗✓
⌃	Lower Largo NO417022	1	1,400	Primary	240m below	Sandy.	✓✓✓✓✓✓✓✓
⌃⌃ ⌃	Upper Largo NO427025					Sandy	✗✗✓
f	Shell Bay NO462003	1	100	Primary	At LWM	Sheltered sandy bay.	✓✓✗✗✓✓✓✗
⌃⌃	Elie/Earlsferry NT489998	1	1,500 (summer) 890 (winter)	Septic tank	270m below	Sandy. Storm water outfalls.	✓✓✓✗✗✓✓✓
⌃⌃	Pittenweem NO550022	1		Storm water outfall	At LWM	Rocky. Fishing port.	✓✓✓ ✗✗✗✓
⌃⌃	Anstruther NO564031	1	1,700	Raw	At LWM	Sand and rocks. Improvements planned to transfer flows to treatment works by 1995.	✓✓✓✓✓✓✓✓
⌃⌃ ⌃	Roome Bay, Crail NO618078	1	230	Raw	At LWM	Sand and rocks. Improvements planned to pump flows to new treatment works for 1995.	✓✓✓✓✓✓✓✓
⌃	St Andrews East NO518164	1	12,970	Primary and disinfection	Above LWM	Improvements planned for 1996 when outfall will be relocated.	✓✓✗✗✗✓✓✓

45. ST ANDREWS, FIFE

OS ref: NO5017

St Andrews is a pretty town, home to the oldest university in Scotland. St Andrews is essentially a mediaeval village and has had a savage past mauled in religious wars. It is now world famous for golf, the Royal and Ancient Golf Club dates from the fifteenth century and is the headquarters of world golf and the supreme authority in golfing matters. To the west, overlooked by a monument to the Protestant Martyrs, is a vast flat, sandy beach with Oystercatchers and Sanderlings.

Water quality
Visitors should be aware that there is a stormwater outfall at this beach.

 Bathing safety
Beware of off shore currents.

 Access
From the town of St Andrews.

 Parking
In St Andrews.

 Seaside activities
Sailing.

Wet weather alternatives
St Andrews has much to offer including a Sealife Centre, Crawfor's Art Centre and the British Golf Museum.

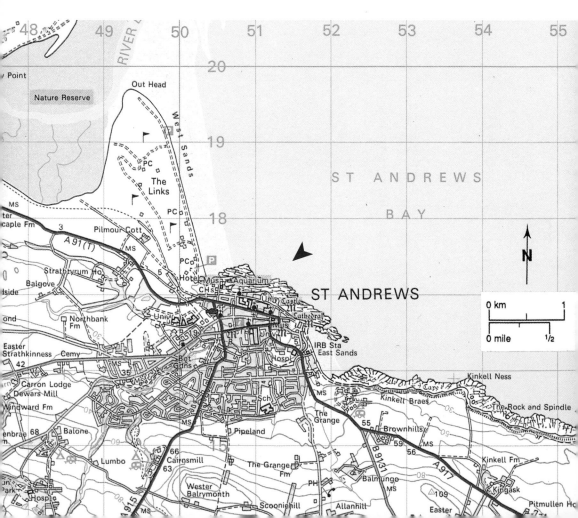

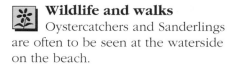 **Wildlife and walks**
Oystercatchers and Sanderlings
are often to be seen at the waterside
on the beach.

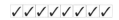

46. TENTSMUIR POINT, FIFE

OS ref: NO5024

A large area of extensive sand dunes north of the Eden Estuary dunes has been stabilised by the conifers planted in the early 1920s by the Forestry Commission. The coastline can still be reached along roads cut through the forest giving access to parking and picnic areas beyond the forest. This is a wild and remote spot with a wide, flat, sandy beach backed by high sand dunes which are continually moving seawards.

Water quality
No sewage is discharged in the vicinity of this beach.

Litter
This beach is sometimes badly littered by marine debris.

Bathing safety
Beware offshore currents.

Access
A turning off the road north-east of Leuchars leads to the forest. There are paths to the beach from the car park.

Parking
There is a Forestry Commission car park behind the dunes.

WC Toilets
At the car park.

Food
None available.

Seaside activities
Swimming.

Wildlife and walks
A large area of the shore, including dunes and developing scrub woodland, is a National Nature Reserve. There is a ranger service based at the car park where a nature trail commences. Wildlife is abundant. The

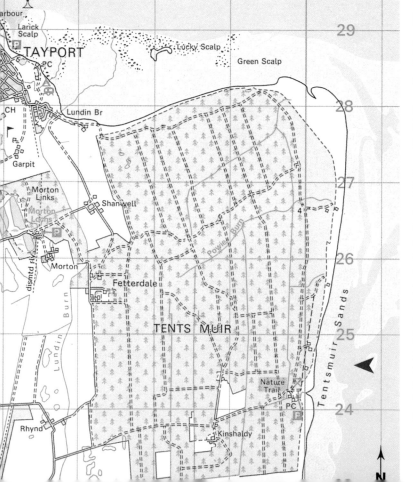

area is a feeding ground for numerous waders and wildfowl and there is rich vegetation. This is an excellent spot for coastal walking with views across the offshore sand banks and away to the Tayside coast.

Track record

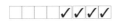

Rating	Resort	Sewage outlets	Population discharging from outlet	Type of treatment	Discharge point relative to LWM (Low Watter Mark)	Remarks	Track record
f	Tayport NO463306	1	3,280	Fine screened	Above LWM		✗✗✗
	TAYSIDE						
⌣⌣	Broughty Ferry NO469306						✗✗✗ ✗✗✓
f	Monifieth NO500320						✗✗✗ ✗✗✗
f	**Carnoustie** NO565343	1	10,200	Screened	Above LWM.	Sandy. Improvements planned to give full secondary treatment by 1999.	✓✓✓✗✗✗✓✗
⌣⌣	**Arbroath** NO630400	2	9,000 21,000	Screened Screened	At LWM 900m below	Red sands. Improvements planned to give full secondary treatment by 2000.	✓✓✗✗✗✗✓✓
⌣⌣ ⌣	Arbroath Victoria Park NO651410						✗✗✓

143

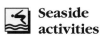 **Bathing safety**
Do not bathe at the mouth of the river, elsewhere bathing is relatively safe.

Access
The shore can be accessed from Lunan.

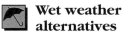 **Parking**
There is limited parking available in Lunan. There is a car park at Boddin Point to the north of Lunnan Bay with a view point.

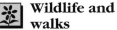 **Seaside activities**
Swimming.

Wet weather alternatives
None available at the beach.

Wildlife and walks
St Cyrus National Nature Reserve to the north is rich in wild flowers, butterflies and moths. Common porpoises are sometimes sighted off the shore and Grey seals are a frequent sight.

Track record

✓ ✓ ✓ ✓ ✗ ✓ ✓ ✓

47. LUNAN BAY, TAYSIDE

OS ref: NO6951

Lunan Bay is an east facing bay north of Dundee. The beach is a broad sweep of sand stretching for 8km (5 miles) divided in two by Lunan Water. On a nearby hilltop, overlooking the beach, is the ruin of Red Castle once owned by Robert Bruce.

Water quality

Rating	Resort	Sewage outlets	Population discharging from outlet	Type of treatment	Discharge point relative to LWM (Low Watter Mark)	Remarks	Track record
⌃⌃	**Montrose** NO728579	2	8,000 6,000	Maceration Screened	Below LWM Below LWM	Sandy. Do not bathe at mouth of river. Improvements planned to give full secondary treatment by 2000.	✔✔✔✔✔✔✔
⌃⌃	Westhaven NO574347						✔✖✔
	GRAMPIAN						
f	St Cyrus NO757648	1	820	Maceration	At LWM	Sand/saltmarsh.	✔✖✖✖✖
⌃⌃	Stonehaven NO891877	2	9,000	Maceration/ primary	Long sea outfall		✔✔✔✔✔✔✔
	Muchalls					Pebbles/rock. Bathing unsafe. Water quality not monitored by RPB in 1993.	
⌃⌃	**Aberdeen/ Nigg Bay** NJ955072						✔✔✔✔✔✔✔
⌃⌃	Aberdeen/ Footdee NJ958060	2	205,060	Screening/ maceration	2.5km below	Sand. New long sea outfall commissioned.	✔✔✔

One of Britain's most extensive sandy beaches stretches south from the River Ythan for 16km (10 miles) down to the River Don on Aberdeen's northern boundary. Fine sand shifts continuously and extensive sand dunes back the beach where shells are plentiful. Towards the southern end at Blackdog there is a rifle range: red flags are raised when in use. This beach is so long that it is seldom crowded, if you are willing to walk you will be rewarded by solitude.

Water quality

There is one outfall in the vicinity of this beach discharging secondary treated sewage below low water mark.

48. BALMEDIE, GRAMPIAN

OS ref: NJ9817

 Litter
Sometimes affected by extensive deposits of marine litter.

Bathing safety
A section of the beach near Balmedie is marked by flags and is patrolled by lifeguards. Swimming is generally safe along the whole of the beach.

Access
The main point of access is at Balmedie which is signposted east from the A92.

Parking
There are several car parks.

 Seaside activities
Swimming.

Wet weather alternatives
Old Slains Castle and Sands of Forvie Nature Reserve Visitor Centre to the north. There are several museums in Aberdeen to the south.

Wildlife and walks
At the northern end of Balmedie Beach is the Sands of Forvie Nature Reserve which is home to Kittiwakes, terns, geese and ducks. The reserve is home to the largest colony of Eider ducks in Britain.

Track record

Rating	Resort	Sewage outlets	Population discharging from outlet	Type of treatment	Discharge point relative to LWM (Low Watter Mark)	Remarks	Track record
⌒⌒	Collieston NK040285	1	200	Maceration	At LWM	Old fishing port.	✓✓✓✓
⌒⌒	Cruden Bay NK090356	1	2,200	Maceration	At LWM	Sand and dunes.	✓✓✗✓✓✓
⌒⌒	Lido Peterhead NK123451	1	20,450	Screened	At LWM	Storm water receives primary treatment. Sand. Emergency outfall only, discharged infrequently.	✓✓✓✓✓✓
⌒	St Combs NK056632					Small fishing port.	✗✓✓✓
⌒	**Fraserburgh** NK005661	12	15,690	Raw	Variable	Sand/dunes. Improvement scheme under way to intercept existing outfalls and provide primary treatment prior to discharge through new long sea outfall. Litter from boats reported on the beach.	✓✓✗✓✓✓✓✓
⌒	Rosehearty NJ933675	1	1,250	Raw		Old fishing port. Golf course. Improvement scheme to intercept and screen existing short sea outfalls under construction.	✓✓✓✓
	Banff Bridge	2	4,420	Raw	Variable	Sand. Improvement scheme under construction to screen effluent prior to discharge. Water quality not monitored by RPB in 1993.	✗✗✗✗✓
⌒⌒	Inverboyndie NJ671646					Long panoramic bay with a good beach. Coastal rangers.	✓✓✓
⌒⌒	Sandend Bay NJ557662	1	280	Settlement		Sandy. Parking for disabled visitors. Good facilities.	✓✓✓
⌒⌒	**Cullen** NJ4480671	2	1,500	Raw	At LWM	Sandy. Golf club nearby.	✓✓✓✓✓✓✓✓
	Findochty	2	1,050	1 raw, 1 macerated	1 at and 1 below LWM	Sand. 2 raw outfalls closed. Water quality not monitored by RPB in 1993.	
⌒⌒	Strathlene, Buckie NJ448671	12	15,000	Raw	Variable	Sand.	
⌒⌒	Lossiemouth East NJ240705	1	42,700	Screens	Via long sea outfall	Sandy.	✗✗✗✓✓✗✓✓
⌒⌒ ⌒	Lossiemouth West NJ212712	2		Raw/ maceration	Short sea outfalls		✓✓✓✓✓✓✓✓
	Hopeman	1	1,663	Raw	At LWM	Rocks just under the water on either side of the bay are dangerous to water users. Sometimes affected by marine litter. Water quality not monitored by RPB in 1993.	
	Burghead	1		Raw	Via long sea outfall east of harbour	Sandy. District Council caravan site nearby. Bathing not recommended. Beach cleaned regularly by the local Community Council.	

Scotland is full of charming, small fishing ports like Keiss Harbour, north of Wick.

Rating	Resort	Sewage outlets	Population discharging from outlet	Type of treatment	Discharge point relative to LWM (Low Watter Mark)	Remarks	Track record
	HIGHLAND						
⌐	**Nairn East** NH893583	2	7,980 220	Primary	Below LWM at far eastern end of beach	Sandy. Improvement scheme to provide secondary treatment and improved storm water management.	✔✔✘✔ ✔✔✔
⌐⌐	Nairn Central	1	180	Septic tank	7m above	Sandy, rock pools at low tide.	✔✔✔✔✔✔✔✔
⌐⌐	Rosemarkie NH7357					No sewage is discharged in the vicinity of this beach. Sand/gravel and shingle. Very popular in summer.	
	Cromarty NH7867	1	200	Raw	Below LWM	Water quality not monitored by RPB in 1993.	
	Nigg Bay					Popular beach in summer. No sewage is discharged in the vicinity of this beach. Water quality not monitored by RPB in 1993.	
	Portmahomack NH915844	1	450	Primary	Below LWM	Sand/dunes. Fishing, sailing and windsurfing popular. Improvement scheme under construction. Water quality not monitored by RPB in 1993.	

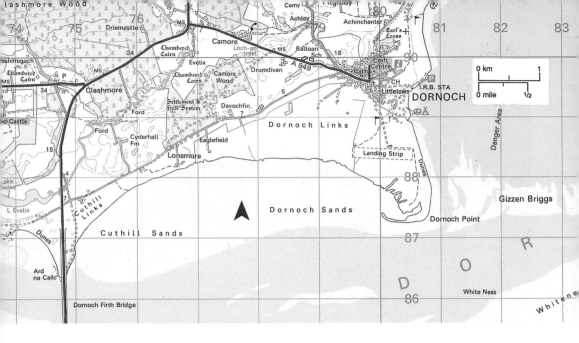

49. DORNOCH, HIGHLAND

OS ref: NH7989

The excellent Royal Dornoch links golf course attracts many visiting players but the lovely sandy beach remains quiet and uncommercialised. The approach to Dornoch is unassuming; the low-lying lands do not permit any view of the beach until you cross the dunes. To the south of the beach is the entrance to the Dornoch Firth which stretches almost 32km (20 miles) inland. The wide sands stretch 5km (3 miles) north narrowing towards Loch Fleet, a small sea loch.

Water quality
No sewage is discharged in the vicinity of this beach.

Bathing safety
There are currents at the northern and southern ends of the beach; safe bathing in the main bay at Dornoch.

Access
From the Square in Dornoch a road leads to the shore and golf courses; another takes you to Embo; there is a short walk across the dunes to the sand.

Parking
There is limited car parking.

Toilets
There is a toilet block at the caravan site backing the beach.

Food
None.

Seaside activities
Swimming, Royal Dornoch Golf Course and Highland Games in August.

Wet weather activities
Dornoch Cathedral. Local social club is open for supervised games during the season.

Wildlife and walks
Loch Fleet, a sea loch at the

northern end of the beach, is the last of the Firth indents into this coastline going north. The loch and the alderwoods behind the mound embankment are nature reserves which contain a wide variety of wildlife. The Scottish Wildlife Trust Reserve Warden runs guided walks in summer.

Rating	Resort	Sewage outlets	Population discharging from outlet	Type of treatment	Discharge point relative to LWM (Low Water Mark)	Remarks	Track record
	Sinclairs Bay, Wick ND3455	5	777	3 primary 2 raw	At LWM	Sandy. New treatment works under construction to replace existing raw outfalls. Water quality not monitored by RPB in 1993.	
	Duncansby Head ND4073					Small, sandy. Water quality not monitored by RPB in 1993. No sewage is discharged in the vicinity of this beach.	
	Dunnet Bay/ Murkle Bay ND2170	2	965 170	Maceration Primary	At LWM Below LWM	Sand and dunes. Water quality not monitored by RPB in 1993.	
⌐	Thurso ND1168	1	9,200	Maceration	At LWM	Sandy. Plans to install screening and primary treatment.	
	Sandside Bay NC9665	1	340	Maceration	Below LWM	Dunes, rocky outcrops. Water quality not monitored by RPB in 1993.	
	Coldbackie NC6060					Sand/dunes. Water quality not monitored by RPB in 1993. No sewage is discharged in the vicinity of this beach.	
	Sango Bay/ Balnakeil Bay NC4068	1	200	Primary	At LWM	Sand/dunes. Water quality not monitored by RPB in 1993.	

Rating	Resort	Sewage outlets	Population discharging from outlet	Type of treatment	Discharge point relative to LWM (Low Water Mark)	Remarks	Track record
	Sandwood Bay NC2165					Sand/dunes. Water quality not monitored by RPB in 1993. No sewage is discharged in the vicinity of this beach.	
	Scourie NC1544	2	200	Primary	At LWM	Sand. Water quality not monitored by RPB in 1993.	
	Clashnessie Bay NC0531					Sand. Water quality not monitored by RPB in 1993. No sewage is discharged in the vicinity of this beach.	
	Clachtoll NC0327					Sand. Water quality not monitored by RPB in 1993. No sewage is discharged in the vicinity of this beach.	
	Achmelvich NC0524					Sand. Water quality not monitored by RPB in 1993. No sewage is discharged in the vicinity of this beach.	
	Achnahaird NC0113					Sand. Water quality not monitored by RPB in 1993. Dunes becoming badly eroded due to visitor pressure. No sewage is discharged in the vicinity of this beach.	
	Achiltibuie NC0109					Shingle. Water quality not monitored by RPB in 1993. No sewage is discharged in the vicinity of this beach	
	Gruinard Bay NG9490					Sand. Water quality not monitored by RPB in 1993. No sewage is discharged in the vicinity of this beach.	
⌢⌢	Gairloch NG7977	4		Primary	All below LWM	Sandy. Safe bathing.	
	Applecross NG7145					Sand. Water quality not monitored by RPB in 1993. No sewage is discharged in the vicinity of this beach.	
	Coral Beaches NG2254					Sand/shells. Water quality not monitored by RPB in 1993. No sewage is discharged in the vicinity of this beach.	
	Morar NM6792	2	100	Raw		New village sewerage scheme including sewage treatment works for 1994. Sand. Water quality not monitored by RPB in 1993.	
	Camusdarrach NM6691					Sand/dunes. Water quality not monitored by RPB in 1993. No sewage is discharged in the vicinity of this beach.	
	Traigh, Arisaig NM6387					Sand/dunes. Water quality not monitored by RPB in 1993. No sewage is discharged in the vicinity of this beach.	
	Sanna Bay NM4469					Sand. Water quality not monitored by RPB in 1993. No sewage is discharged in the vicinity of this beach.	

Rating	Resort	Sewage outlets	Population discharging from outlet	Type of treatment	Discharge point relative to LWM (Low Water Mark)	Remarks	Track record
	STRATHCLYDE						
	Calgary Bay					Sand/dunes. Water quality not monitored by RPB in 1993.	
	Erraid					Sand/dunes. Water quality not monitored by RPB in 1993.	
	Kilchattan Bay	1	170	Raw	At LWM	Water quality not monitored by RPB in 1993.	
	Kames Bay	several	550	Raw		Sand and pebbles. Water quality not monitored by RPB in 1993.	
	Dunoon (West Bay)	1	Unknown	Raw	Below LWM	Sand and pebbles. Water quality not monitored by RPB 1993.	
	Ganavan	1	100	Septic tank	Below LWM	Sand and rocky outcrops. Water quality not monitored by RPB in 1993.	
	Macrihanish	1	200	Raw	At LWM	Sandy. Water quality not monitored by RPB in 1993.	
	Carradale	2	480	Raw	At LWM	Water quality not monitored by RPB in 1993.	
	Helensburgh	1	13,200	Maceration		Sand and pebbles. Water quality not monitored by RPB in 1993.	
	Portkil/Meikleross	1 1	< 100 < 100	Raw Raw	Below LWM Above LWM	Sand and rocks. Water quality not monitored by RPB in 1993.	
	Gourock (West Bay)	4	2,600	Raw	Below LWM	Shingle and rocks. Water quality not monitored by RPB in 1993. Improvement scheme planned.	
	Lunderston Bay	1	Unknown	Septic tank	Above LWM	Shingle and sand. Water quality not monitored by RPB in 1993.	
	Wemyss Bay	3	100 100 11,000	Unknown Unknown Maceration	Above LWM Above LWM Below LWM	Water quality not monitored by RPB in 1993. Shingle and sand.	
	Largs	1	12,000	Unknown	Below LWM	Sand and rocks. Water quality not monitored by RPB in 1993.	
	Fairlie	2	1,000 500	Raw Raw	Below LWM At LWM	Sand and rocks. Improvement scheme planned. Water quality not monitored by RPB in 1993.	
	Millport	11	2,700	Primary	At LWM	Sand and rocks. Reports of gross littering by sanitary towels. Water quality not monitored by RPB in 1993.	
	Seamill	3	4,500	Raw	All at LWM	Sand and rocks. Improvements planned. Water quality not monitored by RPB in 1993.	
	Ardrossan (Boydston)	1	4,000	Maceration	At LWM	Sand and rocks. Improvement scheme in progress. Water quality not monitored by RPB in 1993.	
f	**Saltcoats** NS236420	1	13,500	Screened	Long sea outfall	Sandy.	✔✔✖✖✖✔✖✖

Rating	Resort	Sewage outlets	Population discharging from outlet	Type of treatment	Discharge point relative to LWM (Low Water Mark)	Remarks	Track record
	Stevenston	1	41,000	Screens	1km below	Sandy. Water quality not monitored by RPB in 1993.	
f	**Irvine (Beach Park)** NS236420					Sandy. Improvement scheme completed in 1991.	✗✗✗✗✗✗✗✗
	Gailes	1	100,000	Screens	1.5km	Sandy. Water quality not monitored by RPB in 1993.	
	Brodick Bay	2	1,300	Both raw	1 beyond 1 above	Rocks and sand. Water quality not monitored by RPB in 1993.	
	Lamlash Bay	6	950	Raw	All at LWM	Rocks and sand. Water quality not monitored by RPB in 1993.	
	Whiting Bay	2	800	Raw	Below LWM	Sand and shingle. Water quality not monitored by RPB in 1993.	
	Blackwaterfoot	4	200			Discharges of septic tank effluent. Sand and shingle. Water quality not monitored by RPB in 1993.	
	Troon (North)	1	6,300	Raw	At LWM	Sandy. Improvement scheme under construction – outfall due to be removed by mid 1994.	
⌢	**Troon (South)** NS321307					Sandy.	✓✓✓✓✓✓✓✓
f	**Prestwick** NS345262					Sandy. Sewage related debris a problem.	✓✓✓✗✗✗✗✗
f	**Ayr** NS331219	1	16,200	Screens	140m	Sandy, improvements planned.	✓✓✓✗✗✗✗✗
	Doonfoot	1	8,000	Maceration	220m	Sand/rocks. Improvements planned. Water quality not monitored by RPB in 1993.	
	Butlins (Heads of Ayr)	1	8,500	Secondary	Below LWM	Sandy. Water quality not monitored by RPB in 1993.	
	Maidens	1	600	Primary	At LWM	Sandy and rocks. Improvement scheme planned. Water quality not monitored by RPB in 1993.	
f	**Turnberry** NS199058	1		Primary	Beyond LWM	Sand and rocks. Improvement scheme under consideration.	✓✓✗ ✗✗✗✗
⌢	**Girvan** NX182974	3	4,000 500 2,500	Screens/ maceration Tidal tank Tidal tank	10m below At LWM At LWM	Improvement scheme in progress. Sandy.	✗✗✗✓✗✓✗✓
	DUMFRIES AND GALLOWAY						
⌢⌢	Stranraer Marine Lake NX053615	1	10,000	Primary	10m below	Area affected by silt and effluent from local creamery. Improvements planned to incorporate secondary treatment by the end of 1998.	☐☐☐☐☐✗✗✓

Rating	Resort	Sewage outlets	Population discharging from outlet	Type of treatment	Discharge point relative to LWM (Low Watter Mark)	Remarks	Track record
f	Stranraer Cockle Shore NX080620					Fine sand/silt. Creamery effluent discharged to beach.	✓✓✓
🐦🐦🐦	Portpatrick Outer Harbour NW999539	1	600	Raw	Above LWM	Rocky. Improvement scheme to provide primary treatment by the end of 1994.	✓✓✓
	Portlogan Bay	1	75	Primary	200m below HWM	Sandy. Water quality not monitored by RPB in 1993.	
🐦🐦🐦	Drummore NX135369	2	280 50	Primary		Sandy at the edge of Luce Bay.	✓✓✓
	Ardwell Bay	1	75	Primary	75m below HWM	Sand/shingle. Water quality not monitored by RPB in 1993.	
🐦🐦🐦	Sandhead NX103501	1	250	Raw	Above LWM	Some contamination by animal faeces. Sandy. Improvement scheme to provide primary treatment by the end of 1994.	✗✓✓
🐦🐦🐦	Monreith NX308392					Affected by sea-borne litter, especially after winter storms, although cleared for holiday season. Sand.	✓✓
🐦🐦	Mossyard NX552518					Sand.	✓✓✓
🐦🐦🐦	Carrick Shore NX575498					Fine sand.	✓✓✓
🐦🐦🐦	Brighouse Bay NX636455	1	400	Secondary	30m below	Sandy. Strong tides and rocky shores outside bay.	✓✓✓
🐦🐦	Dhoon NX657486	2	6,000 200	Primary	Primary	Fine sand/silt.	✓✓✓
🐦🐦	Rockcliffe NX894537	2	200 300	Seconary	Secondary	Fine sand	✗✗✓
🐦🐦	Sandyhills NX892551	1	220	Secondary	To tidal watercourse	Fine sand. Sometimes affected by livestock faeces from inland.	✓✓✓✓✗✓✓✓
	Southerness	1	3,500	Primary	500m above	Sand/rock. Water quality not monitored by RPB in 1993.	
f	Powfoot NY147654	1	400	Primary		Silty	✓✗✗
f	Annan NY198649	1	7,900	Primary	Above LWM	Unsuitable for bathing, due to deep channel and nearby Annan sewage outfall. Improvement planned to provide secondary treatment by 2000.	✗✗✗

CHAPTER EIGHT

WALES

THIS CHAPTER COVERS ALL THE BATHING WATERS IN WALES THAT ARE IDENTIFIED UNDER THE
EC BATHING WATER DIRECTIVE AND MANY BEACHES WHICH ARE NOT IDENTIFIED UNDER THE
TERMS OF THE DIRECTIVE. MANY OF THE MORE REMOTE BEACHES HAVE NOT BEEN INCLUDED
SINCE THEY ARE NOT MONITORED BUT ARE STILL DEFINITELY WORTH A VISIT.

•

The coastline of Wales is spectacular. Sand dunes of Anglesey, pounding surf on the Lleyn, kilometres of sand, cliffs and secluded coves of West Wales, the meandering estuaries, and the beautiful Gower peninsular – this is the coast of Wales. There are many

lovely beaches which are comparable with the best anywhere in the country, with the added advantage of not being too crowded. Unfortunately there are individual beaches throughout the region that have failed to meet even the minimum EC standard for bathing water due to the discharge of sewage. This is a problem which is being addressed. Dwr Cymru (Welsh Water), the private water company responsible for sewerage in Wales, announced a major step forward in thinking in 1993. They announced that they would be aiming to treat fully all sewage discharges to at least secondary level with tertiary treatment where necessary. This is something that the other water companies would do well to emulate.

This will not solve all the problems of Welsh beaches though. The north and south coasts suffer from the close proximity of large industrial centres. Swansea, Cardiff, Port Talbot and Newport all contribute to the pollution of the south coast with discharges of domestic and industrial waste. The north coast is affected by pollution from Merseyside and the Wirral. Milford Haven has suffered oil pollution problems from the terminals and refineries that line its shore, and has also suffered from the effects of the antifoulants used on the oil tankers. The best clean and unspoilt beaches are to be found further west, away from the centres of population, and many are certainly worth exploring.

ABOVE: Fall Bay, The Gower.

Rating	Resort	Sewage outlets	Population discharging from outlet	Type of treatment	Discharge point relative to LWM (Low Watter Mark)	Remarks	Track record
	CLWYD						
	Point of Ayr Lighthouse					Water quality not monitored by NRA in 1993	✓✗
⌒⌒	**Prestatyn** SS054839	1	16,246	Screens/ maceration	1km below	Sandy. Safety patrols. Linked to Rhyl scheme. Primary treatment to be provided by 2000.	✗✓✓✓✗✗✓✓
	Ffrith					Sandy. Water quality not monitored by NRA in 1993.	
f	**Rhyl** SJ002826	1	22,600	Maceration/ tidal tank	Long sea outfall	Sandy. Safety patrols. Bathing safe in shore except near river mouth. Sewage-related debris sometimes a problem. Primary treatment to be added by 1995.	✗✗✗
⌒	**Kinmel Bay (Sandy Cove)** SH978866					Sandy. Bathing safe except near river mouth. Linked to Rhyl scheme for completion in 1995.	✗✗✗✗✗✗✗✓
	Abergele (Towyn)	1	4,237	Screens/ maceration/ tidal tank	100m above	Sand/shingle. Linked to Rhyl scheme. Water quality not monitored by NRA in 1993.	✗✓✓
	Abergele (Pensam)	1	7,487	Screens/ maceration/ tidal tank	100m above	Sand at low tide. Linked to Rhyl scheme. Water quality not monitored by the NRA in 1993.	
	Llandulas	1	1,550	Screens/ maceration/ tidal tank	75m below	Sand/shingle. Storm overflow on beach. Linked to improvement scheme at Colwyn Bay. Water quality not monitored by the NRA in 1993.	✓✓✗
f	**Colwyn Bay** SH858791						✓✓✓✓✓✓✓✗
f	Colwyn Bay (end of Cayley Promenade)						✗✓✗
⌒⌒	Colwyn Bay (opposite Rhos Abbey Hotel)	1	25,800	Screens/ maceration/ tidal tank	1km below	Primary treatment by 2000.	✓✓✓
	GWYNEDD						
f	Penrhyn Bay		3,500	Screens/ maceration/ tidal tank	100m above	Sand/shingle.	✗✗✗
f	**Llandudno** SH791822					Sandy.	✓✓✓✓✗✓✗✗
f	**Llandudno (West Shore)** SH765816	1	34,000	Screens/ maceration/ tidal tank	Long sea outfall	Sand/shingle. Complaints due to unsatisfactory discharge in Conwy Estuary. Storm water outfall onto beach.	✗✗✗✗✗✗✗✗
f	Deganwy (North)					To be linked to Llandudno for primary treatment by 2000.	
⌒	Penmaenmawr (Conwy Bay)	1 2	3,700 160	Maceration Raw	200m above 200m above	Sand/shingle Improvements planned.	✗✓ ✓
f	Llanfairfechan					Beware tidal currents.	✓

157

Rating	Resort	Sewage outlets	Population discharging from outlet	Type of treatment	Discharge point relative to LWM (Low Watter Mark)	Remarks	Track record
	ANGLESEY						
	Beaumaris					Shingle/sand. Bathing dangerous on the ebbing tide. Water quality results not available.	
	Red Wharf Bay					Bathing unsafe on ebbing tide. Sewage debris and litter left by users a problem. Water quality not monitored by NRA in 1993.	☐☐☐☐☐✓☐☐
⌒	**Benllech** SH526825						✓✗✓✓✗✗✓✓
	Craig Dwllan (Benllech)	1	2,284	Raw	200m below	Sandy. Long sea outfall planned.	
	Moelfre (Treath Lligwy)	1	894	Raw	100m below	Shingle. Water quality not monitored by NRA in 1993.	
	Amlwch (Bull Bay)	1	4,200	Raw	50m below	Outfall 400 m east of bay (to be extended). Storm overflow below LWM. Water quality not monitored by NRA in 1993.	
	Cemaes Bay	1	1,000	Maceration/ tidal tank	70 m below	Sandy. Water quality not monitored by NRA in 1993.	
	Newry Beach, Holyhead	5	11,000	Raw	All above LWM	Docks area. Water quality results not available.	
⌒	**Trearddur Bay** SH255789			Screening and disinfection		Sand and rocks.	✗☐✓✓✓✓✓✓
	Traeth Llydan (Broad Beach)					Dunes. Water quality not monitored by NRA in 1993.	
⌒⌒	**Rhosneigr** SH323721	1	1,532	Raw	150m below	Outfall discharges from rocks. Many watersports. Enhanced treatment to be provided by 1995 subject to planning approval.	☐☐☐✓✓✓✓✓
	Aberffraw Bay	1	534	Screens/ maceration	At HWM	Sandy, avoid the estuary area as tide ebbs. Extensive dune system. Water quality not monitored in 1993.	
⌒	Llanddwyn					Sandy.	☐☐☐☐☐☐☐✓
	St George's Pier Menai Bridge					Water quality not monitored by NRA in 1993.	☐☐☐☐☐☐✗✓
	Porth Dinorwic Sailing Club (Menai Straits)					Water quality not monitored by NRA in 1993.	☐☐☐☐☐☐✗✗
	Plas Menai (Menai Straits)					Water quality not monitored by NRA in 1993.	☐☐☐☐☐☐✓✓
⌒⌒	**Dinas Dinlle** SH434566					Safe bathing except at the northern end of the beach. The beach is cleaned regularly over the summer, however medical waste has been found on the beach over 1993.	☐☐✓✓✓✓✓✓
	Pontllyfni					Sandy. Water quality not monitored by NRA in 1993.	☐☐☐☐☐☐☐✓

Rating	Resort	Sewage outlets	Population discharging from outlet	Type of treatment	Discharge point relative to LWM (Low Water Mark)	Remarks	Track record
	Trefor	1	582	Secondary	At LWM	Sand/shingle. Water quality not monitored by NRA in 1993.	✓
	Porth Nefyn	1	2,800	Maceration	At HWM	Sand. Surfing, boating. Water quality not monitored by NRA in 1993.	✓
	Morfa Nefyn	1	2,100	Maceration	At LWM	Sand/rocks. Water quality not monitored by NRA in 1993.	✓✓✓
⌒⌒	Porth Dinllaen					Sand/rocks.	✗✓✓✓
	Rhos-y-Llan	1	420	Primary	Off rocks.	Sandy. Water quality not monitored by NRA in 1993.	
	Traeth Penllech					Wide sandy arc.1 km.Good surfing conditions. Water quality not monitored by NRA in 1993.	
	Porth Colman					Rockpools. Water quality not monitored by NRA in 1993.	✓✓
	Porth Iago					Sand. Surfing. Water quality not monitored by NRA in 1993.	✓✓✓
	Porthor	1	Public toilets	Primary		Beautiful sandy cove surrounded by rocky promontories. Water quality not monitored by NRA in 1993.	✓✓✓
	Aberdaron	1	194	Primary	Into River Daron	Sandy. Surfing. Toilets and Cafés. Litter collection in the summer. Water quality not monitored by NRA in 1993.	✓✓✓
	Porth Neigwl Beach					Surfing beach. Strong Atlantic rollers. Also called Hell's Mouth. Water quality not monitored by NRA in 1993.	✓✓
	Porth Ceriad Beach					Water quality not monitored by NRA in 1993.	
	Machroes Beach, Abersoch					Water quality not monitored by NRA in 1993.	
⌒	**Abersoch** SH316277	1	1,356	Secondary	100m below	Sandy.	✓✓✗✓✓✓✓
	Afon Soch at Slipway				.	Water quality not monitored by NRA in 1993.	✓✓
	Llanbedrog	1	672	Maceration/tidal tank	50m below	Sandy. Water quality not monitored by NRA in 1993.	✗✗✗✓
⌒⌒	**Pwllheli** SH371340	1	4,107	Maceration/tidal tank	At harbour mouth.	Sandy.Long sea outfall planned by 2005. Fast currents.	✓✓✓✓✓✓✓
	Morfa Aberech					Sandy. Water quality not monitored by NRA in 1993.	
	Afon Wen	1	46	Maceration/tidal tank	At LWM	Sand/shingle. Water quality not monitored by NRA in 1993.	
⌒	**Criccieth** SH503387	1	800	Tidal tank	50m below	Sand/shingle. Full treatment to be installed by the end of 1995. Littering by sewage debris a persistent problem.	✓✗✓✗✗✓✗✓

Rating	Resort	Sewage outlets	Population discharging from outlet	Type of treatment	Discharge point relative to LWM (Low Water Mark)	Remarks	Track record
⌢⌢	**Black Rock Sands (Morfa Bychan)** SH542359	1		Maceration	3km below	Windsurfing and surfing.	☐☐☐☐☐✓✗✓
	Morfa Bychan	1	800	Maceration	Long sea outfall	Sandy beach. Contaminated by local streams. Do not bathe at SE end. Litter frequent but is collected daily. Water quality not monitored by NRA in 1993.	✗✗✓✓✓✓✓☐
⌢⌢	**Harlech** SH567314	1	1,291	Primary	At LWM	Sandy beach. Outfall to be extended and provided with screening.	✓✓✓✓✓✓✓✓
⌢	**Llandanwg** SH566281	1	258	Primary	At LWM	Sand/rock. Bathing safe at high tide.	✓✓✓✓✓✓✓✓
⌢⌢	Tal-y-Bont					Sand, dunes.	☐☐☐☐☐✓✓✓
	Llanaber (Dyffryn)					Smuggling village. Water quality not monitored by NRA in 1993.	☐☐☐☐☐☐✓✓
⌢⌢	**Barmouth** SH608159	1	2,200	Screened	Long sea outfall	Sandy. Estuary unsafe for swimming. Good area for walking.	✓✓✓✓✓✓✓✓
⌢⌢	**Fairbourne** SH609130	1	474	Tidal tank	400 m below	Sandy. Starting point of the smallest narrow gauge railways. Improvements under review.	✓✓✓✓✓✓✓✓
	Llwyngwril	1	370	Raw	At LWM	Sand/shingle. Water quality not monitored by NRA in 1993.	☐☐☐☐☐☐✗✗
⌢	**Tywyn** SH576003	1	2,811	Maceration/ tidal tank	Above LWM	Sandy. Surfing. Secondary treatment and disinfection by 1996.	✗✓✓✓✓✓✓✓
f	**Aberdyfi** SN607958	1	6,000	Primary/ tidal tank	At LWM	Sewage outfall in estuary. To be combined with Tywyn scheme.	☐☐✗✗✓✗✗
	DYFED						
	Ynyslas (North)					Water quality not monitored by NRA in 1993. 3km long sandy beach around the dunes of the National Nature Reserve at Ynyslas down to Borth.	☐☐☐☐☐☐✓
	East Tywyni, Ynyslas						☐☐☐☐☐☐✓
⌢⌢	**Borth** SN606901					Bathing dangerous near mouth of the estuary. Dog by-laws in force.	✓✓✓✓✓✓✓✓
	Clarach Bay						
f	South of River					Affected by discharges from nearby caravan parks.	☐☐☐✗✗✗✗✗
f	North of River						☐☐☐☐☐☐✗✗
⌢	**Aberystwyth North** SN583822						✓✓✓✓✓✓✓✓
f	Aberystwyth Harbour						☐☐☐☐☐✗✗✗
f	**Aberystwyth South** SN579814	1	9,100	Screened		Secondary treatment works, UV disinfection and outfall planned for 1995.	✗✗✓✗✗✓✗✗

Rating	Resort	Sewage outlets	Population discharging from outlet	Type of treatment	Discharge point relative to LWM (Low Watter Mark)	Remarks	Track record
⌒	Tanybwlch Beach, Aberystwyth						✔✔✔
⌒⌒	Morfa Bychan Beach (Slipway)					Rocky beach in break in cliffs. Difficult access via steep ramp.	✔✔✔
⌒⌒	Llanrhystud	1	500	Primary		Shingle. Sand at low tide.	✔✔✔
⌒⌒	Llansantffraid	1	1,160	Primary	At LWM	Sand and shingle.	✔✔✔
⌒	Llanon Slipway					Access to beach by foot only.	✔✔
⌒⌒	Aberarth	1	470	Primary	At LWM	Shingle beach.	✔✔✔
⌒⌒	Aberaeron North of outfall						✗✔✔
⌒⌒	Fourth Groyne North Harbour	1	5,000	Raw	At LWM	Sand and shingle. Primary treatment by 2000.	✔✗✔
⌒	Little Quay Bay (Central Groyne)					Sand.	✔✔✔
	New Quay						
⌒	New Quay (Centre)						✔✗✔
⌒⌒	New Quay (South)						✔✔✔
⌒	**New Quay (Traeth Gwyn)** SN398597	1	6,000	Maceration	1.3km below	Long sea outfall off Llanina Point. Primary treatment by 1995.	✔✔✔✔✔✔✔
⌒⌒	Cwmtydu					Secluded shingle and sand. Remains of lime kiln on beach.	✗✔
⌒⌒	Llangrannog	1	400	Primary	75m below	Sand/shingle. Lifeguards patrol from July to September.	✗✗✔✔
⌒⌒	Penbryn					Sand.	✗✔✔
⌒⌒	Tresaith	1	180	Maceration	75m below	Sand and shingle. Lifeguards.	✗✔✔✔
⌒	Aberporth Beach East						✗✗✔✔
⌒	Aberporth at Slip	1	1,842	Maceration	75m below	Sandy. Lifeguards patrol from 11 July to 5 September. Sewage-related debris a problem. Improvement plans to install assisted primary treatment and disinfection by microfiltration by 1996.	✗✗✔

161

50. MWNT, CARDIGAN, DYFED

OS ref: SN1952

Anatural suntrap and surrounded by National Trust land, this beautiful undeveloped sandy beach is quite easily accessible and can be very popular in summer. The 300m (330 yards) of gently sloping sands are fringed by folded and faulted shale and mudstone cliffs. The beach is shadowed by the imposing form of Foel-y-Mwnt, a conical hill on the headland. The tiny whitewashed church of The Holy Cross nestles in a hollow at its foot. The only other obvious sign of man is the remnant of a lime kiln adjacent to the path down to the beach; limestone was landed in the bay and fired ready for use by the local farmers. Dogs are banned from May to September.

Water quality
No sewage is discharged in the vicinity of this beach.

Bathing safety
Bathing is safe inshore. Care is required as surface currents, due to waves breaking on the headland, deflect across the bay. There is an emergency phone on cliff path.

Access
Mwnt is signposted from the B4548 north of Cardigan. Lanes lead to car park above the beach. Steps and a steep path lead down to the beach.

Parking
There is a National Trust car park with 250 spaces.

WC Toilets
There are toilets at the head of the steps to the beach, with facilities for disabled visitors.

Food
Refreshments are available from Easter to October.

Seaside activities
Swimming.

Wildlife and walks
National Trust cliff-top walks. A pack detailing walks in the Cardigan area is available from local tourist information centres. Foel-y-Mwnt hill on the headland provides good views of the bay south to Cardigan Island and the narrow rocky inlet to the

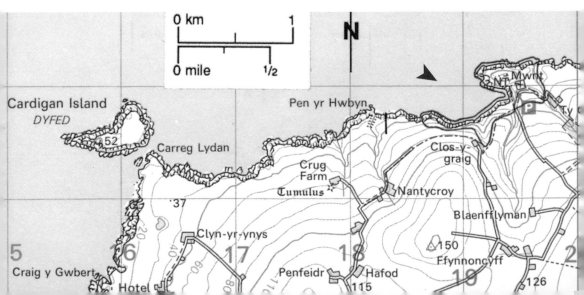

north. On the cliff tops above the beach there is a small remnant dune system where Marram grass covers the wind-blown sand. Dogs on leads are welcome on the footpaths.

Track record

Rating	Resort	Sewage outlets	Population discharging from outlet	Type of treatment	Discharge point relative to LWM (Low Watter Mark)	Remarks	Track record
	Gwbert-on-Sea					Affected by discharges from caravan park and private properties. Water quality not monitored by NRA in 1993.	✘✘
	Poppit Sands						
↷↷	West SN152489						
↷↷	East SN156492			Secondary		Sand and shingle. Estuary polluted by outfalls at Cardigan. Bathing safe only at slack water and where there are lifeguard indicators.	
f	**Newport** SN053407						✓✓✓✓✓✓✓✘
↷↷	Newport Sands South SN052405	1	1,400	Maceration LWM	500m below	Bathing safe in centre of beach except on ebb tide or when rough. Sand/shingle.	
↷	Pwllgwaelod SN003399	1	880	Secondary	At LWM	Grey sand.There is a wheelchair link to Cwm-yr-Eglwys for disabled visitors.	
	Fishguard					Linked to Goodwick.Water quality not monitored by NRA in 1993.	
↷	Goodwick Harbour (South) SM948381						✓ ✓
↷↷	Goodwick Sands SM949379	1	2,710	Raw	At LWM	Ferry terminal. Complaints of sewage in water. Outfall to be extended and treatment added. Water quality not monitored by NRA in 1993.	✓✓ ✓
↷↷	Abereiddy Bay (at slipway) SM796312						✓✓✓

51. WHITESANDS BAY, ST DAVID'S, PRESELI, PEMBROKESHIRE

OS ref: SM7327

Gorgeous sunsets framed in the wide arc of Whitesands Bay, from the remote rocky headland of St David's to St John Point, are an added attraction of this lovely beach. There are splendid views away to Ramsey Island and the Bishops and Clerks; the South Bishop can be identified on the far horizon by its lighthouse. The wide white sands stretch for 1.6km (1 mile). Large pebbles are thrown to the top of the beach by the waves that frequently crash on to this beach, much to the delight of many surfers. Open fields slope down to the shore from the imposing craggy hill Carn Llidi, which provides good walking with excellent sea views. St David's Head is owned by the National Trust. There is a dog ban from May to September.

Water quality
No sewage is discharged in the vicinity of this beach.

Litter
The beach is rarely littered and is cleaned regularly.

Bathing safety
There are dangerous and unpredictable currents off parts of the beach and at some states of the tide. Warning signs indicate where to bathe. Flags indicate when it is safe. Lifeguards patrol the beach during the summer. There are Weever fish at the beach. Power boats are restricted to 8 knots within the bathing area.

Access
A road off the A487 north of St David's, signposted to Whitesands, leads directly to car park adjoining the sand. This beach is suitable for wheelchair users and other people with mobility difficulties.

Parking
There is a car park behind the beach, with approximately 400 spaces.

Toilets
There are toilets at the car park.

Food
There is a café/shop at car park.

164

Seaside activities

Swimming, surfing and canoeing. There is zoning of activities when the beach is busy.

Wildlife and walks

The coast path north provides an interesting circular walk, taking in St David's Head with the remains of a fort and a burial chamber, and returning round Carn Llidi Hill. A guide describing the route is published by the Pembrokeshire Coast National Park and can be obtained at information offices locally. Ramsey Island lies just south of the bay, and boat trips from Whitesands (12-person inflatables, May-September) take you round the island to view the seabird breeding colonies.

Track record

✓✓✓✓✓✓✓

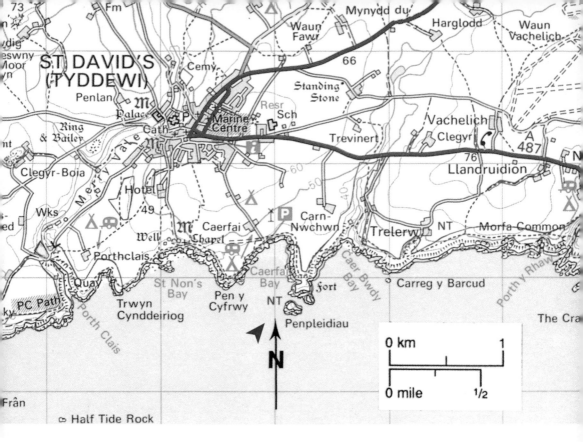

52. CAERFAI BAY, PEMBROKESHIRE

OS ref: SM 7524

Caerfai is a popular bathing beach near St David's. At high tide the beach consists entirely of rocks and boulders but at low tide sand is revealed. The cliffs in the bay are impressive but very unstable and should be treated with caution. It is possible to explore a number of the caves in the area but be careful and keep an eye on the tide. To be safe, check the tide times.

Water quality
No sewage is discharged in the vicinity of this beach.

Bathing safety
Generally safe.

Access
Caerfai is signposted from the A487 east out of St David's.

Parking
There is a car park above the beach with a short and very steep footpath to the beach.

WC Toilets
There are no toilets available at the beach; the nearest facilities are in St David's.

Food
The nearest refreshments available are in St David's.

Seaside activities
Swimming and rockpooling.

Wet weather alternatives
St David's is the smallest city in Britain. There is a secluded cathedral

founded by St David in the sixth century. The present cathedral was begun in the twelth century, and is built from purple stone from Caerbwdi Bay. Ruins of the Bishop's Palace stand in the cathedral grounds.

53. NEWGALE SANDS, PEMBROKESHIRE

OS ref: SM8422

Newgale is a highly popular beach because of the sweeping expanse of sand and ease of access to the beach. The beach is backed by a pebble bank and at high tide the sea may come right up to the bank and the whole beach may disappear. Newgale is west facing and so is open to swells coming in from the Atlantic, making it very popular with surfers.

Water quality
There is no sewage discharged in the vicinity of this beach.

Bathing safety
There are areas set aside for swimmers, please stick to these areas as there can be unpredictable currents and undertows at some states of the tide. Lifeguards patrol in the summer.

Access
Follow the A487 Haverfordwest – St David's Road. This passes directly alongside the northern end of the beach. To get to the beach you have to walk across the pebble bank which has matting across it in places.

Parking
There are three car parks at intervals along the road.

Toilets
There are toilets at the north end of the beach.

Food
There are shops, a pub and a café at the north end of the beach.

Seaside activities
Swimming and surfing. Surf boards can be hired.

Rating	Resort	Sewage outlets	Population discharging from outlet	Type of treatment	Discharge point relative to LWM (Low Watter Mark)	Remarks	Track record
⌒⌒	**Broad Haven** SM861138	1	2,200	Secondary	At HWM	Sandy. Surfing only possible on big swells. Good area with easy access for windsurfing, particularly wave sailing. Winds exposed.	✗✓✓✓✓✓✓✓
	St Brides Haven					Popular area with divers. Many rockpools. Water quality not monitored by NRA in 1993.	☐☐☐☐☐☐☐✓
	Musselwick Sands					Water quality not monitored by NRA in 1993. Cliff backed cove. Take care – it is possible to get cut off by the rising tide.	

 Wet weather alternatives

None.

 Wildlife and walks

At extremely low tides the remains of a prehistoric forest are exposed. Walkers should take care at either end of the beach as it is possible to get cut off.

Track record

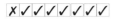

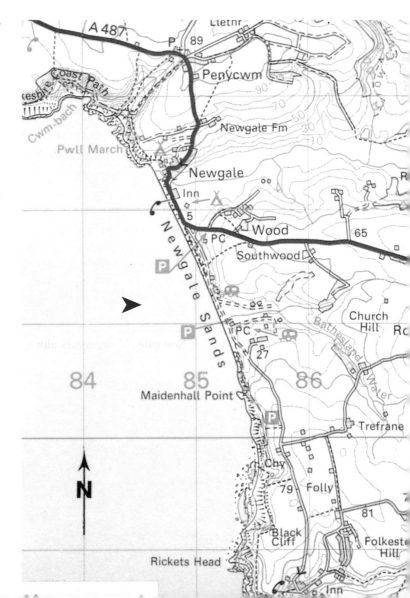

54. MARLOES SANDS, MARLOES, PRESELI, DYFED

OS ref: SM7908

Magnificent Marloes is a 1.6km (1 mile) stretch of wide flat golden sands which reaches from the imposing bulk of Gateholm Island in the north-west to Red Cliff and Hooper's Point to the south east. Beds of rock laid flat on a seabed long ago are tilted and seem to be pushing up through the sands. Their jagged outlines point skywards along the length of this glorious bay. The steep cliffs that bound the beach reflect these dipping strata; do not attempt to climb them as they are dangerous. The barnacle and seaweed-covered rocky outcrops testify to the fact that the whole beach disappears at high water. There is only one access point to the beach where a tiny stream flows through a narrow valley, so take care not to get cut off at the extremities of the beach by the incoming tide.

Water quality
No sewage is discharged in the vicinity of this beach.

 Bathing safety
Beware of currents and rock. There is some lifesaving equipment available. Take care as some areas of the beach are quickly cut off by the rising tide.

 Access
From Marloes village a lane, signposted Marloes Sands, takes you to the National Trust car park.

P Parking
National Trust car park with about 50 spaces, and see map.

WC Toilets
None.

Seaside activities
Swimming and fishing.

Wildlife and walks
The coast path that follows the cliff top round the bay provides excellent views of the sands. There is a 3km (2 mile) nature trail starting from the National Trust car park. To the south west, the coast path leads to West Dale Bay and a series of secluded sandy beaches around the Dale Peninsula that can only be

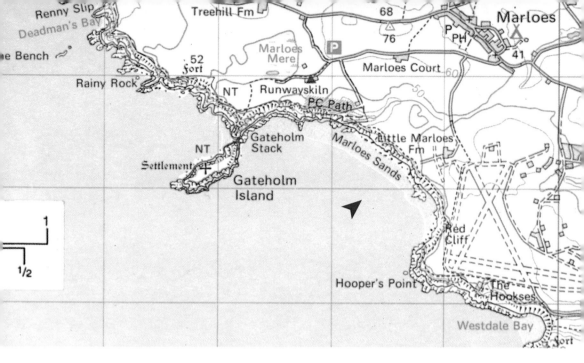

reached on foot. To the north-east, the path heads to Albion Reach and Martin's Haven. Boat trips run from Martin's Haven to Skomer Island, renowned for its seabirds, wildflowers and seal colonies, and a marine area now a designated Marine Nature Reserve.

Track record

Rating	Resort	Sewage outlets	Population discharging from outlet	Type of treatment	Discharge point relative to LWM (Low Watter Mark)	Remarks	Track record
⌒	Dale SM813058	1	600	Maceration/ tidal tank	Above LWM	Shingle/sand. Protected site for windsurfing. Shop. RYA tuition available. Reports of sewage when wind is onshore.	✓✓ ✓
	Sandy Haven	1	1,360	Secondary	At LWM	Red sand. Water quality not monitored by NRA in 1993.	
	Milford Beach					Near major refinery town. Water quality not monitored by NRA in 1993.	
	Neyland Slip					Shingle bank. Water quality not monitored by NRA in 1993.	
⌒⌒	Angle Bay SM852033	1	500	Secondary	At LWM	Shingle and muddy sand.	✓
⌒	Broad Haven (South Beach) SR979939					Sand, dunes. Popular with surfers. Although this beach fulfils the requirements for a Guideline pass of the EC Bathing Water Directive. It has failed the Mandatory standard at some stage over the season and so cannot be recommended.	✓

171

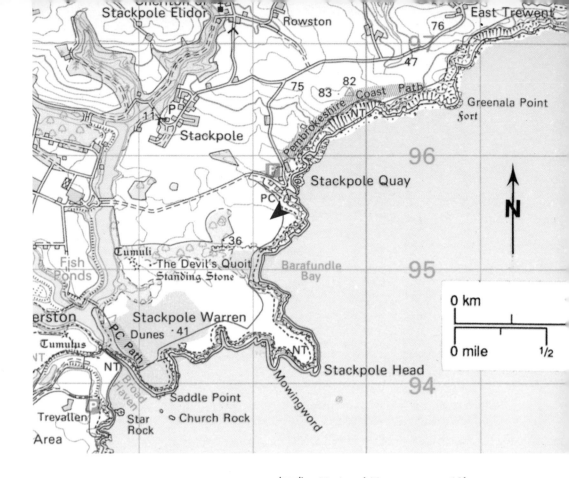

55. BARAFUNDLE BAY, STACKPOLE, PEMBROKESHIRE

OS ref: SR9995

The National Trust owns a 13km (8 mile) section of the coast around Stackpole, including the beautiful Barafundle Bay. The beach can only be reached by foot with a 1.6km (1 mile) walk along the cliff top from Stackpole Quay. One of many tiny harbours that once proliferated in West Wales, the stone quay in this tiny inlet has been restored by the National Trust. From the clifftop path you get your first glimpse of the bay, an impressive view of soft golden sands backed by high dunes, with steep limestone cliffs rising on either side. The cliffs, with distinctive dark bands at their base due to the encrusting seaweeds, barnacles and lichens, extend to Stackpole Head which shelters the bay.

Water quality

No sewage is discharged in the vicinity of this beach.

Litter

The beach is generally clean. A small amount of litter is washed up by the tide. In summer the beach is cleaned daily by the National Trust.

Bathing safety

Bathing is safe. There is lifesaving equipment at top of steps down the cliff.

Access

A lane east of Stackpole, signposted to Stackpole Quay and Barafundle, leads to the car park at Stackpole Quay. A ten-minute walk along the coast path, signposted from the car park, leads to the bay; follow the steps down the cliff to reach the sands.

Parking

There is a National Trust car park at Stackpole Quay with about 230 spaces.

Toilets

There are toilets at the car park.

Food

None.

Seaside activities

Swimming.

Wildlife and walks

The coast path from Stackpole Quay crosses the beach and, climbing through the trees, the path tracks around Stackpole headland, passes Rame Blow Hole, and continues on to Broadhaven Bay. There are excellent views of the rocky coastline, and north-east the ranks of red sandstone headlands extend to the horizon. Walking south-east there are views down on to tiny sandy coves which cannot be reached because of the steep limestone cliffs that tower above.

Track record

Rating	Resort	Sewage outlets	Population discharging from outlet	Type of treatment	Discharge point relative to LWM (Low Water Mark)	Remarks	Track record
⌐	Freshwater East SS019979	1	600	Raw	At LWM	Sandy. Although this beach meets the requirements for a Guideline pass of the EC Bathing Water Directive it has failed the Mandatory standard at some stage over the season.	✓✓ ✓

56. MANORBIER BEACH, PEMBROKESHIRE

OS ref: SS0597

Manorbier has been described as the most delectable spot in Wales, and perhaps this description is not too far off the mark. The village of Manorbier is very picturesque and the beach itself is very popular with bathers and surfers. Although the beach is mainly sandy there is a pebble bank at the high tide line. The water can get very crowded when the surf is good.

Water quality
There is one outfall discharging secondary treated sewage from 520 people.

Bathing safety
There can be a dangerous undertow in rough sea so take care. Basic lifesaving equipment is available above the beach.

Access
The beach is signposted from the village of Manorbier which is off the B4585 and lies between Pembroke and Tenby. The roads are narrow so drive carefully.

Parking
There is a pay and display car park owned by the National Trust above the beach.

Toilets
There are toilets in the car park.

Food
There are shops and pubs in the village.

 Seaside activities
Swimming and surfing.

Wildlife and walks
The area around Manorbier is steeped in history and is well worth exploring. Manorbier Castle and church date from the twelfth century and overlook the beach. To the south of Manorbier Bay is a burial chamber, King's Quoit, which is about five thousand years old.

Track record

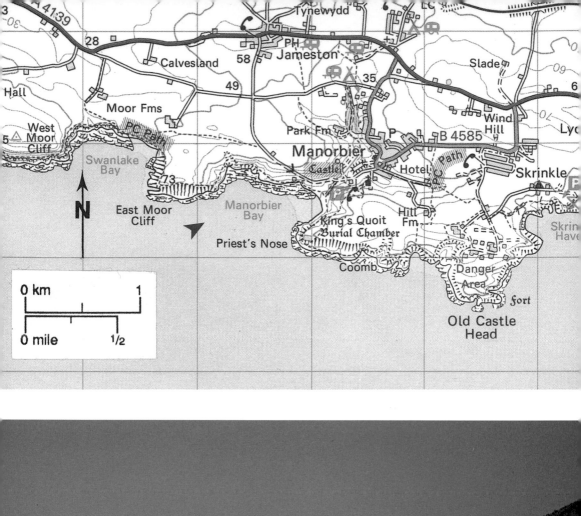

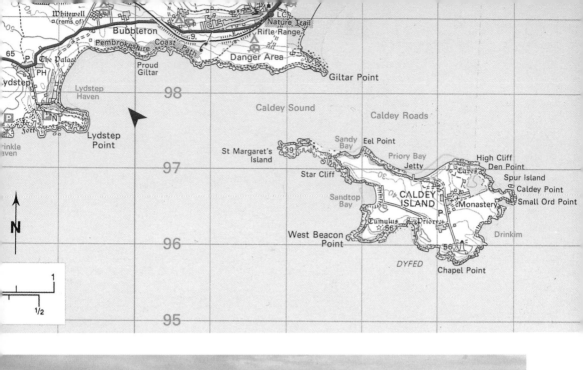

57. LYDSTEP HAVEN, PEMBROKESHIRE

OS ref: SS0998

Lydstep Haven is a very pretty privately owned beach consisting of sand and pebbles backed by impressive wooded cliffs at either end and by a large caravan park in the middle.

Water quality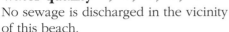
No sewage is discharged in the vicinity of this beach.

Bathing safety
Bathing generally safe.

Litter
The beach is regularly cleaned.

Access
There are two points of access to the beach. The first is via a private road off the A4139 through the caravan site to the beach (an admission charge is levied) and the second is via a rough track from Lydstep village.

Parking
There is plenty of parking above the beach if the route via the caravan is taken.

Toilets
There are toilet facilities available, including a dog loo.

Food
There are shops and cafés at the beach.

Seaside activities
Lydstep has all the usual seaside attractions. Bikes and deckchairs can be hired.

Wildlife and walks
Lystep Caverns can be explored when the tide is out, Smugglers Cavern can be reached at all states of the tide. Lydstep Point to the south is owned by the National Trust and there are good views of Caldey Island.

Rating	Resort	Sewage outlets	Population discharging from outlet	Type of treatment	Discharge point relative to LWM (Low Watter Mark)	Remarks	Track record
	Tenby						
∩∩	**North** SN134008						✓✗✓✓✓✓✓
∩∩	**South** SS132998	1	25,000	Screened/maceration	2.7km below	Sandy. Highly effective beach management team on North Beach. Primary to be provided by 2000.	✗✗✓✓✓✓✓✓
	Saundersfoot						
∩	Beach SN141047	1	11,000	Primary	50m below	Sand and shingle. Sewage-related debris reported. Flows to be transferred to Tenby.	✓✗✓✓✓✗✓
∩∩	**Amroth** SN167068					Sand and shingle. At very low tides the remains of drowned forest can be found in the sand.	✓✗✓✓✓✓✓
∩∩	**Pendine Sands** SN238074					Sand and dunes. Part of beach often closed for MOD firing range.	✓✓✓✓✓✓✓

58. PEMBREY SANDS, LLANELLI, DYFED

OS ref: SN3802

A marvellous beach with 12km (8 miles) of sand edged by a belt of sand dunes, known locally as Cefn Sidan. The beach falls within the Pembrey Country Park which also covers the extensive grassland and forest behind the dunes. The middle of the beach near the visitors' centre can be very busy on a warm sunny afternoon, but the extremities remain relatively quiet although they are often used for marine sports. Land yachting by the local club is well-worth watching. Whether you want to relax on the sand and enjoy the clear views to the Gower on the horizon, or be more active, the country park has lots of facilities, both natural and man-made, to keep the whole family happy. Dogs are not permitted in the central section of the beach, and this rule is enforced by the rangers and lifeguards.

Water quality
There is one outfall discharging secondary treated sewage serving 2,500 people.

Litter
Flotsam and jetsam are washed up on this beach. This may be on the increase, but it is cleaned daily.

Bathing safety
Bathing is safe. Lifeguards patrol the beach near the main access point from May to September.

Access
The country park signposted from the A484. Board walks from the car parks lead through the dunes to the beach.

Parking
There are several car parks behind dunes with about 1,000 spaces.

Toilets
There is one toilet block with facilities for disabled visitors. There are three other sets of toilets in the country park.

Food
There is a permanent kiosk with outdoor seating, providing snacks and drinks.

Seaside activities
Swimming, windsurfing, sailing and fishing. Pitch and putt golf, miniature and narrow gauge railways, adventure play area and dry ski slope. Events are regularly staged on the beach; for example, sand sculpture competitions and treasure hunts.

Wet weather alternatives
Kidwelly Castle and Industrial Museum, Pembrey Motor Sports Centre. The Country Park Information

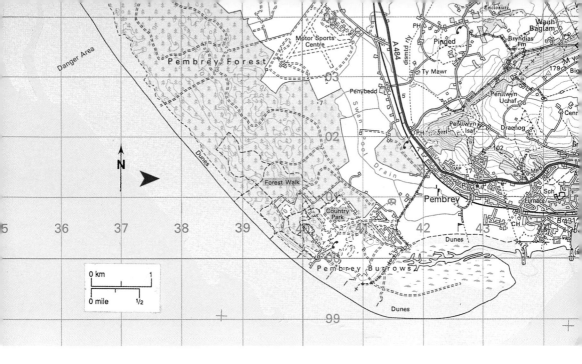

Centre presents displays and exhibitions about the beach and country park (open all year).

🌼 Wildlife and walks

The area is a Site of Special Scientific Interest. There are four self-guided nature trails around the country park: woodland walk, floral trail, the yellow post walk (which includes the beach, dunes, forest and grassland), and the leisure route, suitable for wheelchairs and pushchairs. There is a permanent orienteering course, a programme of guided walks by the ranger service and a nature quiz for children. Full information is available from the visitors' centre.

Track record

✓✓✓✓✓✓✓

Rating	Resort	Sewage outlets	Population discharging from outlet	Type of treatment	Discharge point relative to LWM (Low Watter Mark)	Remarks	Track record
⌐	Burry Port Beach East SN446002	1	6,000	Primary	Below LWM	Industrial and muddy. Bathing unsafe. Linked with Llanelli scheme for secondary treatment and disinfection to be provided.	✓✓✓
f	Llanelli Beach (Fourth Groyne) SS496995					See above for treatment.	✗✗✗
WEST GLAMORGAN							
⌐⌐	Broughton Bay SS419930					Sandy, bathing unsafe.	✓✓

59. RHOSSILI BAY, RHOSSILI, WEST GLAMORGAN

OS ref: SS4287

A spectacular 5km (3 mile) sweep of golden sands edges Rhossili Bay, stretching from Worms Head north to Burry Holms. The sands are shadowed by Rhossili Down; its grass slopes rise 200m (656ft) above the beach and are popular with hang gliders. The southern end of the beach is ringed by steep cliffs which fall away northwards, where the Down is replaced by sand dunes. Worms Head, contrary to its name, is in fact an island, only linked to the mainland at low tide. The remains of a wreck can sometimes be seen at low tide. This lovely beach and the adjacent Down are owned by the National Trust.

Water quality

There is one outfall serving 380 people discharging primary treated sewage. Complaints of visible sewage have been received which may be linked to animal faeces washed from the north Gower marshes.

Litter
Considerable quantities of marine litter, such as fishing gear, get washed up on the beach.

Bathing safety
The beach is usually safe for bathing. However, sand banks sometimes build up causing dangerous rip currents in rough conditions.

Access
The B4247 leads to Rhossili village. There is a good path down the cliffs to the beach. This beach has a slipway which makes access to the beach easier for wheelchair users and people with mobility difficulties.

Parking
There is a car park in village.

Toilets
There are toilets at the car park.

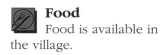 Food
Food is available in the village.

Seaside activities
Swimming, surfing (extremely popular) and fishing.

Wildlife and walks
Worms Head island and the adjacent stretch of coast are a National Nature Reserve. The limestone cliffs are rich in flora, and nesting birds can be seen on the nature trail. The limestone rocky shore of the Gower is one of the best examples in Britain. There is a network of paths on the headland and the adjoining Down where superb views can be obtained.

Track record

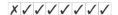

Rating	Resort	Sewage outlets	Population discharging from outlet	Type of treatment	Discharge point relative to LWM (Low Watter Mark)	Remarks	Track record
	Fall Bay	1		Primary		South of the Worms Head. Access difficult. Water quality not monitored by NRA in 1993	✔
	Ramsgrove	1	270	Primary	Below LWM	Sandy. Water quality not monitored by NRA in 1993.	

60. PORT EYNON, WEST GLAMORGAN

OS ref: SS4685

The rocky headland to the south, Port Eynon Point, shelters this sandy cove. The road from the post office leads down to the shore where a short section of newly built promenade gives access to the beach. On either side, high dunes back the wide, flat sands. High cliffs rise on either side of the bay with rocky outcrops at their base. On the eastern side of the bay stand the newly excavated remains of a salt house and workings. The wide, gently sloping sands are safe for bathing, and an ideal spot for building sand castles or playing cricket. A dog restriction by-law is being considered.

Water quality ⌒⌒⌒⌒⌒

One outfall serving 1,200 people discharges primary and secondary treated sewage at low water mark off Overton Mere, east of Port Eynon Point.

Litter

The beach is cleaned daily in summer and twice weekly in winter.

Bathing safety
Warning notices indicate where it is safe to bathe. The beach is patrolled by lifeguards from 1 May until 31 August.

Access
From the village a road leads to main access point where there is direct level access to the sands via board walks and marked paths through dunes. This beach has a slipway which makes access to the beach easier for wheelchair users and people with mobility difficulties.

Parking

There is a car park behind the dunes with 500 spaces.

Toilets

There are toilets at the beach entry point.

Food

There is a shop and café at the beach entrance.

Seaside activities

Swimming, surfing, windsurfing, diving, canoeing and fishing. A boat ramp leads from the car park to the tidal sand, providing easy access to the beach for boats.

Wildlife and walks

The South Gower Coast Nature Reserve stretches from Port Eynon to Worms Head at Rhossili, comprising 10km (6 miles) of rocky shore with faulted and folded grey limestone cliffs. There is a most interesting limestone flora, and nesting birds can be seen on some ledges. The limestone rocky shore of the Gower is one of the best examples in Britain. There is a footpath onto Port Eynon Point which climbs the cliff from the eastern end of the beach. The path leads to the Culver Hole, a deep cleft in the cliff which has been sealed off with a wall. There is a nature trail from the Rhossili Bay car park at the opposite end of the Nature Reserve.

Track record

✓ ✓ ✓ ✓ ✓ ✓ ✓

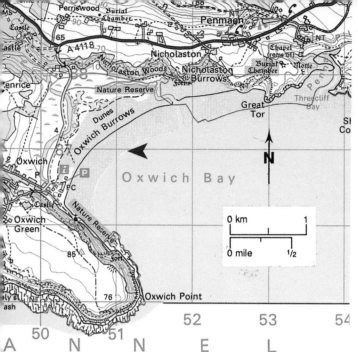

Water quality

No sewage is discharged in the immediate vicinity of this beach.

Bathing safety

Bathing is safe.

Access

Narrow lanes lead to Oxwich village at the western end of the bay, and a car park next to the dunes faces directly on to the beach. A ramp for launching boats can be used for easier access to the hard intertidal sand. There is also access to the other end of the beach: a fifteen-minute walk from Penmaen along the footpath marked Tor Bay leads to a steep path down the cliff.

Parking

Large car park at Oxwich village, plus limited parking at Penmaen. In summer there is a National Trust car park (a farmer's field) at Penmaen.

Toilets

There are two toilet blocks at the Oxwich car park.

Food

The Oxwich Bay Hotel at the eastern end of the beach provides meals and bar snacks. There is a kiosk for refreshments at the car park, and cafés and a shop in the village.

Seaside activities

Swimming, windsurfing, sailing, diving, canoeing and fishing. A slipway across the sand enables boats to be launched and makes the bay popular with waterskiers. There is a windsurfing school on the beach.

61. OXWICH BAY, OXWICH, WEST GLAMORGAN

OS ref: SS4986

A superb beach; from the steep tree-clad slopes of Oxwich Point a sweep of very fine soft sand backed by high dunes curves 3km (2 miles) round the bay to Great Tor – a stretch of towering rocky limestone cliffs. At low tide wide, flat sands are revealed. There is only one indentation into the crescent of sand, where the dunes are interrupted by the river Nicholaston Pill which meanders through marshland before crossing the beach. The main access is from Oxwich village where there are full facilities. The North Devon Coast can be seen on the horizon and in the evening it appears as a string of lights. At low tide Oxwich Bay links with Three Cliffs Bay to the east, giving 5km (3 miles) of continuous south-facing sands.

✿ Wildlife and walks

The Oxwich National Nature Reserve covers most of the beach, back-shore and the Oxwich Point headland. The reserve includes a wide variety of habitats: sandy beach, dunes, saltwater and freshwater marshes, cliffs, woods and grassland. There are marked footpaths throughout the reserve, and board walks give access to the dunes. A path west of the hotel leads through the trees past St Illtyd's Church to steps which climb to the headland and along the coast to Horton. There is an interpretative centre at the car park at Oxwich. At the western end there are barnacle- and mussel-encrusted rocks below the cliffs, and low tide reveals pools teeming with life.

Track record

✓✓✓✓✓✓✓

Rating	Resort	Sewage outlets	Population discharging from outlet	Type of treatment	Discharge point relative to LWM (Low Water Mark)	Remarks	Track record
⌐	Three Cliffs Bay SS535876					Sandy. Although this beach fulfils the requirements for a Guideline pass of the EC Bathing Water Directive it has failed the Mandatory standard at some stage over the season.	▢▢▢▢▢▢✔
	Southgate	1	500	Secondary	Below LWM	Rocky. Water quality not monitored by NRA in 1993.	
	Brandy Cove	1	2,000	Secondary	Below LWM	Rocky. Former smugglers stronghold. Water quality not monitored by NRA in 1993.	▢▢▢▢▢▢✔
⌐⌐	**Caswell Bay** SS591874 **Langland Bay**					Sandy. Surfing safe except on ebb tide. Effective beach management. See Swansea Bay.	✔✘✔✔✔✘✔
f	**West**					Sandy. See Swansea Bay. Popular surfing beach.	✘✔✔✘✔✔✘
⌐	**Limeslade Bay** SS6255870					Sandy. See Swansea Bay.	✘✘✔✘✔✔✔
⌐	**Bracelet Bay** SS630871					Sandy. See Swansea Bay.	✔✔✔✔✔✔✔

Rating	Resort	Sewage outlets	Population discharging from outlet	Type of treatment	Discharge point relative to LWM (Low Water Mark)	Remarks	Track record
	Swansea Bay						
f	**The Mumbles** SS644921						✗✗✗✗✗✓✗✗
🐦🐦	Knap Rock SS625878						✗✓✓
f	Opposite Black Pill Rock SS632898						✓✓✗
f	Mumbles Head Pier SS632874	1	170,000	Screened/tidal tank	Below LWM	Subject of many complaints about marine litter and sewage debris. New projects for whole bay area, but not due until 1997, covering Swansea, Bracelet, Limeslade, Langland, Caswell and Oxwich Bays.	✗✗✗
🐦	Jersey Marine, nr Swansea. SS704925						✓✓✓
🐦	Jersey Marine East SS709916						✓✓
🐦🐦	Jersey Marine West SS692920						✗✓
	Baglan (Neath)	1	60,000	Screened	3.1km below	Improvements planned to give secondary treatment by 2000. Water quality not monitored by NRA in 1993.	
	Afan (Port Talbot)	1	60,000	Screened	2.4km below	Improvements planned to give secondary treatment by 2000. Water quality not monitored by NRA in 1993.	
🐦🐦	**Aberafan** SS739896						✗✗✓✓✗✓✓✓
🐦🐦	Aberafan, West SS728906						✓
	Margam Sands (opposite steel works).					Access difficult. 5km stretch of sand. Good surfing. Water quality not monitored by NRA in 1993.	✓✓
	MID GLAMORGAN						
🐦🐦	**Rest Bay** SS800779					Sand and rocks. Surfing popular. Lifeguards.	✗✓✓✓✓✓✓
	Porthcawl					Sand and rocks. Sewage transferred to Penybont treatment works at Ogmore by Sea. Water quality not monitored by NRA in 1993.	
🐦🐦	**Sandy Bay** SS824765					Sand and rocks. Surfing popular. Lifeguards. Bathing prohibited either side of the beach.	✗✗✗✓✗✓✓✓

Rating	Resort	Sewage outlets	Population discharging from outlet	Type of treatment	Discharge point relative to LWM (Low Watter Mark)	Remarks	Track record
⌒⌒	**Trecco Bay** SS831763					Sand and rocks. Surfing. Lifeguards. Bathing prohibited either side of the beach.	✗✗✗✔✗✔✔✔
	Newton Bay (Newton Point)					Water quality not monitored by NRA in 1993. Sand and rocks. Powerboating. Bathing prohibited at Newton Point	✗
	Ogmore by Sea	1	140,000	Secondary/ other	Into River Ogmore approx 1.6km from sea	Sand and rocks. Lifeguards. Bathing prohibited near estuary. Water quality not monitored by NRA in 1993.	✗✗✗✔
⌒	**Southerndown, (Dunraven Bay)** SS884729					Sand and rocks. Strong currents off Trwyn y Witch headland, bathing prohibited. Lifeguards. Heritage Coast visitor centre nearby.	✗✔✗✔✔✔✔✔
	SOUTH GLAMORGAN						
	Nash Point					Rocky. Bathing unsafe. Water quality not monitored by NRA in 1993.	
	Tresilian Bay	1	8,000	Maceration	At LWM	Rocky. Bathing unsafe. Water quality not monitored by NRA in 1993.	
⌒⌒	Llantwit Major Beach SS955673					Easy access to a stretch of sand and shingle. Good walks on headlands either side of bay.	✗✔✔
	Limpert Bay	1	4,500	Maceration	At LWM	Rocks, shingle and sand overlooked by power station. Water quality not monitored by NRA in 1993.	✔
⌒⌒	Font-y-Gary Bay	2	3,045 936	Raw Raw	At LWM At LWM	Rocky, difficult currents. Lifeguards. Sewage to be transferred to Barry West, long sea outfall planned.	✔✗✔✔
⌒⌒	Watch House Bay, Barry						✔✔✔
⌒⌒	Little Island Bay, Barry						✔✔✔
⌒⌒	**Cold Knap Beach** ST096664	1	23,000	Screening	Long sea outfall 1.5km below	Pebbles and sand. Lifeguards. New scheme to transfer sewage to Barry West proposed for completion in 1997, with Whitmore and Jacksons Bay.	✗✗✗✔✗✔✔✔
⌒	**Whitmore Bay Central** ST114662	2	21,000 23,000	Maceration Raw	At LWM At LWM	Sand, shingle and mud. Beach patrolled.	✔✗✔
⌒	Jacksons Bay ST122665					Sandy, falling rocks at back of beach. Lifeguards. Sewage to be transferred to Barry West. Reports of litter.	✗✗✗✗✗✗✗✔
⌒	St Mary's Well					Shingle and rocks.	✗✗✗✔
f	Penarth	4				Shingle and rocks. Bathing dangerous.	✗✗✗

CHAPTER NINE

NORTHERN IRELAND

THE COAST OF NORTHERN IRELAND REMAINS LARGELY UNDISCOVERED TO THOSE OUTSIDE THE
PROVINCE ALTHOUGH ITS MOST FAMOUS FEATURE, THE GIANT'S CAUSEWAY, IS ONE OF THE
NATURAL WONDERS OF THE WORLD. THE CAUSEWAY CONSISTS OF HUGE BASALT COLUMNS THAT
DISAPPEAR INTO THE WAVES LIKE A STAIRWAY TO THE DEPTHS.

•

The whole coast has a rich and varied geology with a succession of bays and rugged
headlands. The strands of County Londonderry have popular holiday resorts, and the
nine glens of County Antrim, each with a little beach nestling at its mouth provide a
quieter alternative. There are also the magnificent sea loughs of County Down: Belfast,
Strangford and Carlingford, rich in wildlife and scenery. It is unfortunate that undiscovered
does not mean unthreatened: Strangford Lough has suffered from the effects of scallop
dredging in recent years. Dredging for scallops may not necessarily affect the quality of the
beaches but the damage to such a beautiful and unique habitat should concern anyone
who cares for our coasts and coastal life. The implementation of an effective management
plan is essential to maintain the balance in Strangford Lough. The issues concerning the
Lough are being widely discussed and debated, progress is being made, but the problem
won't solve itself.

LEFT: The Giant's Causeway, Northern Ireland.

Rating	Resort	Sewage outlets	Population discharging from outlet	Type of treatment	Discharge point relative to LWM (Low Watter Mark)	Remarks	Track record
⌐	**Benone** C723362					Long sandy beach. Although this beach fulfils the requirements for a Guideline pass of the EC Bathing Water Directive it has failed the Mandatory standards at some stage over the season and so cannot be recommended.	☐✔✔✔✔✔✔
⌐	**Castlerock** C777364	1	1,060	Maceration	At LWM	Sandy. Sewage-related debris sometimes a problem.	☐✘✔✔✔✔✔
⌐⌐	**Portstewart** C808367	1	6,040	Maceration	Above LWM	Miles of sandy beach. This area is owned by the National Trust and a leaflet with further information is available from them.	✔✔✔✔✔✔✔
⌐	**Portrush Curran Strand** C863318					Although this beach fulfils the requirements for a Guideline pass of the EC Bathing Water Directive it has failed the Mandatory standards at some state over the season and so cannot be recommended. Sometimes affected by sewage-related debris.	✔✔✔✔✔✔✔

62. MILL STRAND, PORTRUSH, CO. ANTRIM

OS ref: C8740

Portrush is the largest and most popular seaside holiday centre in Northern Ireland. This Victorian and Edwardian resort is located on rocky Ramore Head and has all the facilities and amusements that might be expected of a traditional holiday town. From its elevated position there are excellent views along the coast to Donegal in the west and Rathlin Island in the east. A low sea wall bounds the soft sands of the west bay which curves gently south from the small harbour. The promenade which runs along the sea wall is on two levels separated by grassy banks. The larger East or Curran Strand is also backed by a sea wall but this gives way to dunes and a links golf course.

Water quality
One outfall serving 5,000 people discharges macerated sewage at low water mark.

Bathing safety
Beware of currents that may affect bathing safety.

Access
Steps and a ramp from the promenade.

Parking
150-200 spaces at West Strand, 250-300 at East Strand.

Toilets
There are toilets for men and women at each end of West Strand and on East Strand.

Food
Promenade café.

Seaside activities
Swimming, surfing, windsurfing, sailing, diving and fishing. Boat trips from the harbour.

Wet weather alternatives
Water World alongside the old harbour has a swimming pool

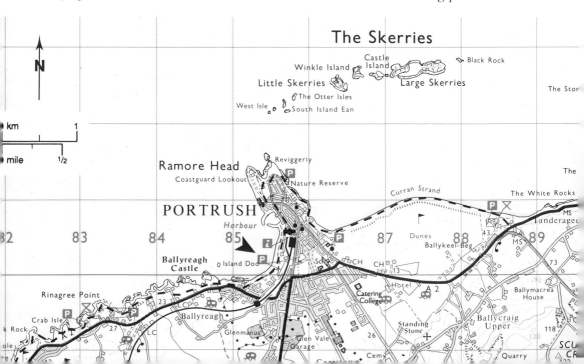

complete with flumes and jacuzzis. Its facilities include an aquarium and light entertainments. Amusements.

🌼 Wildlife and walks

A section of the rocky shore on the eastern side of Ramore Head between the Portandoo Harbour and Bath Road is a Nature Reserve noted for its fossil ammonites. Adjacent to the reserve is the Portrush Countryside Centre, an interpretative centre which can provide further information about the reserve and surrounding area. East of Portrush there is superb cliff scenery, including towering limestone cliffs eroded by the waves to form arches and caves. The white cliffs are replaced by the brown basalt which forms the famous Giant's Causeway further east. Leaflets about the area are available from the National Trust. The coastal path follows the clifftop to the

picturesque ruin of Dunluce Castle which offers superb views along the coastline (the castle is closed on Sunday mornings and on Mondays during the winter).

Track record

Rating	Resort	Sewage outlets	Population discharging from outlet	Type of treatment	Discharge point relative to LWM (Low Watter Mark)	Remarks	Track record
⌒	**Ballycastle** D123412	1	3,920	Maceration	At LWM	Sandy.	✗✓✓✓✓✓✓
	White Park Bay					Sandy, dunes. Water quality not monitored by DoE-NI in 1993.	
⌒	**Browns Bay** D436028					Sandy. Safe swimming. Although this beach fulfils the requirements for a Guideline pass of the EC Bathing Water Directive it has failed the Mandatory standards at some state over the season and so cannot be recommended.	✓✓✓✓✓✓✓
⌒⌒	**Helen's Bay** J460829	1	1,600	Tidal tank	At LWM	Sandy. Safe swimming.	✓✓✓✓✓✓✓
f	**Crawfordsburn** J467826	1	1,200	Secondary	Discharges to stream	Sandy.	✓✓✓✓✓✓✗
⌒	**Ballyholme** J518824					Sandy.	✗✗✓✓✓✓✗✓
⌒	**Groomsport** J450836	1	40,000	Screened	At LWM	Sandy.	✓✓✗✓✓✓✓✓
⌒⌒	**Millisle** J601757	1	1,000	Primary	At LWM	Sandy.	✓✓✓✓✓✓✓

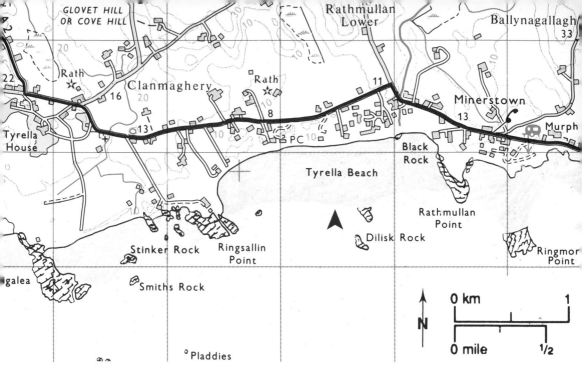

63. TYRELLA BEACH, CLOUGH, CO. DOWN

OS ref: J4535

Situated in Dundrum Bay, Tyrella is a 5km (3 mile) stretch of unspoilt sandy beach facing south and backed by dunes. The clean, shallow water and safe bathing make this a very popular beach on sunny Sundays in the holiday season: at other times it is blissfully quiet. There are six golf courses within a 20km (12 mile) radius of the beach, including the excellent Royal County Down. There is a tourist information and an interpretation centre next to the toilets.

Water quality
No sewage is discharged in the vicinity of the beach.

Bathing safety
Safe bathing.

Access
The A2 between Clough and Killough passes directly behind the beach.

Parking
At present, some cars do park on the beach: this is a practice of which the Marine Conservation Society strongly disapproves. Alternative parking should be found.

Toilets
A new toilet block has been completed.

Food
Snack vans visit the beach especially during the summer.

Seaside activities
Swimming.

Wet weather alternatives
Leisure centres at Newcastle and Downpatrick, each about 10km (6 miles) away.

192

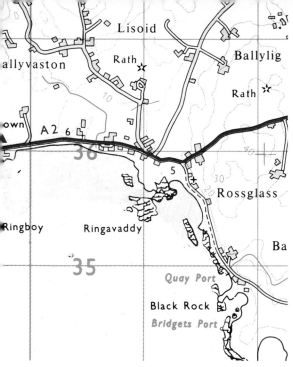

The Murlough Nature Reserve is close by – a dune system with plenty of wildlife and vegetation. There are signs of man's early habitation of the area: castles, dolmens (ancient cairns) and some of the earliest Christian remains (a result of St Patrick landing in the area). The Ulster Way goes past the beach.

Track record

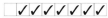

Rating	Resort	Sewage outlets	Population discharging from outlet	Type of treatment	Discharge point relative to LWM (Low Watter Mark)	Remarks	Track record
	Murlough					Sandy. Water quality not monitored by DoE-NI in 1993.	
⌒⌒	**Newcastle** J384318	1	20,000	Secondary	285m below LWM	Sandy. New treatment works should ensure continued compliance in future.	✗✗✗✓✗✓✓✓

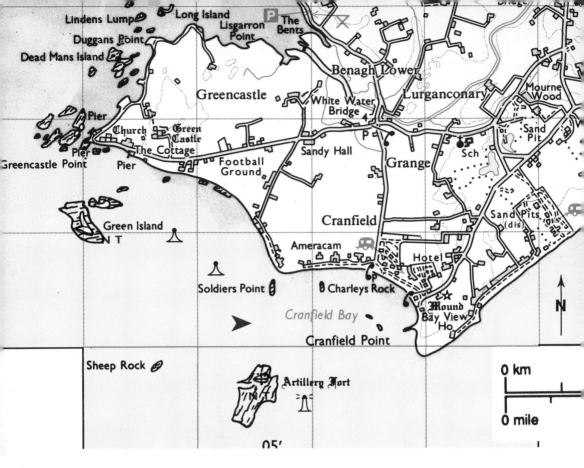

64. CRANFIELD, NICHOLSONS STRAND, KILKEEL, CO. DOWN

OS ref: J2611

An Area of Outstanding Natural Beauty and adjoining an area of Special Scientific Interest, Cranfield Bay is situated at the entrance to Carlingford Lough. The south-facing sand and shingle beach is backed by dunes and has the magnificent Mourne mountains as a backdrop. The beach stretches from the rocky outcrops at Greencastle Point to the boulders at Cranfield Point. There are good views across the Lough to Ballagan Point and away down the coast beyond Dundalk Bay.

Water quality
No sewage is discharged in the vicinity of the beach.

 Bathing safety
Safe bathing.

Access
A road leads from Cranfield to the car park, from which there is a short walk across the grass to the beach.

P Parking
Car park with 150 spaces.

WC Toilets
There are toilets available.

 Food
Hotel, two cafés and three shops.

 Seaside activities
Swimming, windsurfing, diving,

water skiing and fishing. Beach entertainment and band concerts. Golf course.

 Wet weather alternatives
There is the Analong cornmill and a marine park nearby.

Wildlife and walks
Mourne mountains are excellent for walking, with the Silent Valley Reserve just north of Kilkeel. A 14,000 million litre (3,000 million gallon) reservoir is set among the peaks and there is some fine parkland on the approaches to the dam.

Track record

						✓	✓

Rating	Resort	Sewage outlets	Population discharging from outlet	Type of treatment	Discharge point relative to LWM (Low Watter Mark)	Remarks	Track record
↷	**Cranfield Bay** J268105	1	2,200	Fine screens	410m below LWM	Long sandy south-facing beach.	✓✓✓✓✓✓✓

Rating	Resort	Sewage outlets	Population discharging from outlet	Type of treatment	Discharge point relative to LWM (Low Water Mark)	Remarks	Track record
	GUERNSEY						
	Grand Havre					No sewage discharged in the vicinity of this beach. A large sandy beach edged by granite outcrops. Water quality not monitored in 1993.	✔
⌒	Pembroke Beach 341839					Large sandy beach with a narrow band of pebbles near the sea wall. Windsurfing. Although this beach fulfils the requirements for a Guideline pass of the EC Bathing Water Directive it has failed the Mandatory Standard at some stage over the season and cannot be recommended.	
⌒⌒	Havelet Bay 341780					Fort George sewage outlet to the south of the beach. Sandy. Aquarium nearby. Picnic area. Only beach on the island designated for water skiing. Good rockpooling.	✔
⌒⌒	Fermain 339761	1	1,000	Maceration	Discharges 30m from the beach	Popular beach. Pebbles giving way to sand at low tide.	✔✔
	Moulin Huet Bay					Sandy. Fascinating rock formations. Rocky pooling. Café. Steep path to beach. Water quality not monitored 1993.	
⌒⌒	Petit Bot Bay 305749	1	8,000	Maceration/ screening	3km from beach	Pebbles with large expanse of sand at low tide.	✔✔
⌒⌒	L'Eree					No sewage is discharged in the vicinity of this beach. Large sandy beach with good bathing. Prone to seaweed deposits.	✔✔
	Perelle Bay					Sandy. Surrounded by rocks. Not very good for swimming. Water quality not monitored in 1993.	

THE CHANNEL ISLANDS

THE CHANNEL ISLANDS ARE BRITAIN'S MOST SOUTHERLY POINT. THE MAIN ISLANDS ARE GUERNSEY, JERSEY, ALDERNEY, HERM AND SARK. LYING 23KM (14 MILES) OFF THE COAST OF FRANCE IT IS STRANGE TO THINK THAT THE ISLANDS HAVE BEEN BRITISH SINCE THE TIME OF WILLIAM THE CONQUEROR.

•

Beaches on Alderney, Sark and Herm are not included in *The Reader's Digest Good Beach Guide,* however they are fabulous places to visit. Sark is only 5km (3 miles) long and has been a feudal state governed by a Seigneur since 1565. Travel on the island is by bicycle, tractor or horse-drawn carriage – no cars are allowed. Herm is even smaller than Sark measuring in at only 250 hectares (618 acres). Shell Beach at the north of Herm consists of millions of tiny shells, some from as far away as the Gulf of Mexico. There are, not surprisingly, no cars or roads on the island but Herm is home to around a hundred of the famous Guernsey cows.

•

Guernsey itself is a picturesque island with spectacular cliffs and sandy beaches. The capital of Guernsey is St Peter Port which is known as one of the finest harbour towns in Europe. The island has its own government, issues its own coins and stamps but is subject to the Crown. The islanders are English-speaking although French Patois can be heard. The island has had a turbulent history which is reflected in the archaeology which ranges from neolithic remains to Royalist castles and concrete defences constructed by the Germans during the occupation of the island in the Second World War.

Sewage treatment on the island is not exactly ideal. There are three main outfalls and several minor discharges, but there is very little contamination from industrial sources in the island's sewage. There is a dog ban in effect between 1 May and 30 September at all the Guernsey beaches listed.

•

Jersey was established as an independent state over 700 years ago. It originally belonged to Normandy, and so came under the same sovereignty as England in the Norman Conquest. King John lost the island to France in 1204 but the islanders chose to remain loyal and although they are not governed by Parliament they are subject to the Crown.

Jersey is famous for its coastline. It has an excellent record for water quality and has one of the most comprehensive sewage treatment works in Britain. There is full sewage treatment for the island which includes screening, settlement, activated sludge oxidation, secondary treatment and ultraviolet disinfection. Beaches on Jersey are cleaned daily by hand and mechanically. Dogs are banned from the beaches in Jersey between 10.30am and 6pm from 1 May to 30 September with fines for those not complying. Jersey takes care of its beaches, so with 55km (34 miles) of coastline ranging from high cliffs to sweeping bays and bathing waters meeting the highest EC standards Jersey must surely be a destination for the discerning beach lover.

This is only the second year that comprehensive monitoring has been carried out on Jersey and Guernsey and so the track record is for two years only.

LEFT: Herm, The Channel Islands.

65. VAZON BEACH, WEST COAST, GUERNSEY

OS ref: 285798

Vazon Beach is a crescent of lovely clean sand which gets the sun from early morning until sunset. However it is exposed to the wind from most directions.

Water quality

There is no sewage discharged in the vicinity of this beach.

Litter

The beach is cleaned on a daily basis throughout the summer season.

Bathing safety

Safe bathing.

Access

There are slipways at either end of the beach providing disabled access and flights of steps at several other places.

Parking

There is plenty of parking at several car parks immediately above the beach.

Toilets

There are toilets including facilities for disabled visitors at several places along the beach.

Food

There are two beach kiosks and a number of restaurants and hotels in the area.

Seaside activities

Swimming, surfing and windsurfing. All activities are carefully zoned.

Wildlife and walks

The Fort Hommet Nature Conservation Area is found at the northern end of the beach and is of considerable interest historically and for its wildlife.

Track Record

					✓	✓

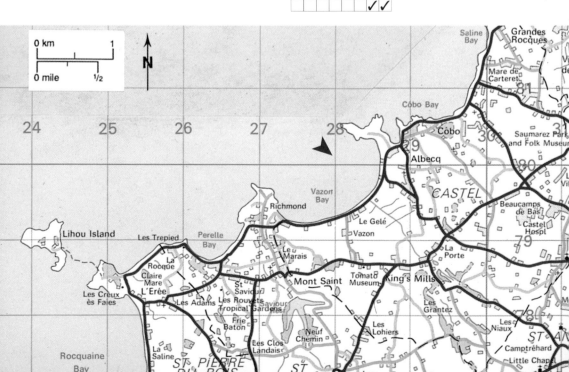

Rating	Resort	Sewage outlets	Population discharging from outlet	Type of treatment	Discharge point relative to LWM (Low Watter Mark)	Remarks	Track record
⌃⌃	Cobo 296809					No sewage discharges in the vicinity of this beach.	☐☐☐☐☐✔✔
	Saline Bay (Grandes Rocques)					Water quality not monitored in 1993. No sewage discharges in the vicinity of this beach. Sandy/shingle. Large rocks. Rock pools.	
⌃	Port Soif 305819					An almost circular very sheltered bay with fine dry sand. Although this beach fulfils the requirements for a Guideline pass of the EC Bathing Water Directive it has failed the Mandatory standard at some stage over the season and cannot be recommended.	☐☐☐☐☐✔✔

66. ST OUEN'S BAY, JERSEY

OS ref: 565514

St Ouen is the longest stretch of beach in Jersey and is locally referred to as the 'five mile' road. As the name suggests, it is a stretch of 5 miles (8km) of sandy beach spanning the length of the west coast. This is a very popular beach for surfing and has been the venue for international surfing competitions. The vast sandy beach is backed by Les Mielles conservation area. Situated to the south of the bay is La Rocco Tower which can be visited at low tide but is cut off at mid to high tide.

Water quality

Every water sample taken over 1993 met the EC Guideline Standards for coliforms and streptococcus. This is truly exceptional water.

Litter

Litter bins are emptied daily between May and September. Dog waste bins are provided.

Bathing safety

This is a popular surfing beach but bathing can be dangerous. The main beach guard headquarters is situated at St Ouen's Bay where there is beach guard cover between late April to the end of September. There are emergency telephones at 7 locations which are linked direct to the headquarters and out of hours to the fire service. There are flagged bathing areas.

Access

There are numerous points of access to the beach by means of slipways and steps.

Parking

There are numerous car parks along the length of the bay and also car parks which have been specially designed to blend in with the surrounding dune area by partially enclosed grass banks.

Public transport

The number 12a bus will take you to St Ouen's Bay.

Toilets

There are toilets at numerous places along the bay with facilities for disabled users. Disabled visitors should obtain a 'Radar' key at the Town Hall (deposit £5) to gain access to cubicles for disabled visitors across the island.

 Food
There are numerous cafés, beach kiosks and also licensed restaurants.

 Seaside activities
Surfing, including instruction and equipment hire. Boogie boarding and land yachting at approved times through the association. There is a nine hole municipal golf course at Les Mielles together with a driving range and crazy golf course.

 Wet weather alternatives
Les Mielles interpretation centre.

 Wildlife and walks
La Mielle de Morville, adjacent to Kempt Tower, is a pleasant place to walk and the starting point for longer circular routes. The sand dunes support over 400 plant species. The Les Mielles conservation area is an area designated to conserve and protect the dune area together with surrounding flora and fauna. There are weekly guided walks around Les Mielles every Thursday afternoon between May to September.

Track record

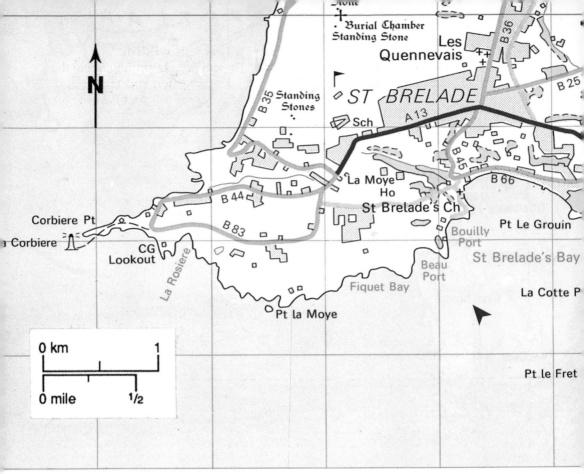

67. BEAUPORT, JERSEY

OS ref: 579479

A beautiful secluded sandy beach on the southern coast of Jersey. The small sandy beach is sheltered by headlands of rock on either side of the beach. This beach is very close to the much larger St Brelade's Bay and offers a much quieter alternative.

Water quality

No sewage is discharged in the vicinity of this beach. Beauport now has a very high standard of water quality despite failing in 1992. The 1992 failure was due to the dumping of several tonnes of potatoes and the subsequent leachate. This problem has been satisfactorily addressed.

Litter
There are bins at the beach which are emptied regularly.

Bathing safety
There is no beach guard cover but bathing is relatively safe.

Parking
Small car park at the top of the path.

Public transport
Take the Number 12 bus, the nearest bus stop is about ten minutes walk away.

Toilets
There are no toilet facilities at the beach.

 Food
Occasionally there is a refreshment van in the car park.

 Seaside activities
Swimming.

 **Wet weather alternatives**
None.

Walks and wildlife
There is a path running along the headland which offers spectacular views of the bay. Beauport is home to the Dartford Warbler.

Track record

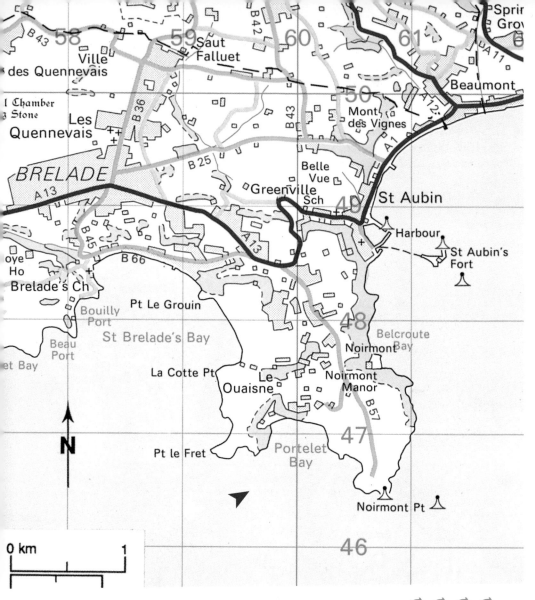

68. PORTELET, JERSEY

OS ref: 600470

This is a quiet sandy beach, popular with the locals, in a sheltered bay situated on the south-west coast of the island. At half to full tide the bay encompasses an attractive island called Janvrin's Tomb.

Water quality

Only one water quality sample failed to meet EC Guideline Standards in 1993. Excellent water quality.

Bathing safety

There is no beach guard cover, however due to the sheltered nature of the bay bathing is relatively safe.

Litter

Litter bins are emptied daily May to September.

Access
Access to the beach is via steep steps with bench seating at three points. This is an unsuitable beach for people with limited mobility.

Parking
There is parking available behind the beach.

Public transport
Bus number 12a.

Food
There is a café selling food and beach goods. There is a newly refurbished bar and restaurant adjacent to the car park.

Seaside activities
There are facilities for hiring deck chairs and windbreaks. This is a particularly good area for exploring rockpools.

Wet weather alternatives
St Aubin Harbour is a short drive away and has many attractive shops and restaurants.

Track record

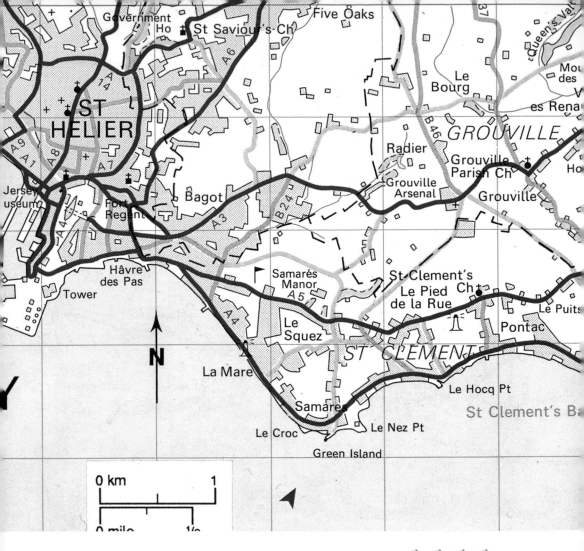

69. GREEN ISLAND, JERSEY

OS ref: 673461

A ten minute drive from the town of St Helier, Green Island is a pleasant sandy beach, popular with locals. There are outcrops of rock and at low tide extensive rockpools are exposed. The actual Green Island is a mound in the sea which can be accessed at low tide but visitors must beware that the Island gets cut off at high tide.

Water quality

Litter
There are litter bins at the beach.

Bathing safety
The bathing is safe but there is no beachguard cover.

Access
There is one main slipway to the beach.

Parking
There is parking available at St Clements.

Public transport
Bus number 1.

 Toilets
There are toilets at the car park.

 Food
Cafés nearby.

 Seaside activities
Swimming.

 Wet weather alternatives
St Helier, the capital, is nearby.

 **Walks and wildlife**
Green Island is too popular for shore birds to be in evidence, however walking east towards Le Hocq the coastline provides an excellent habitat for shore birds.

Rating	Resort	Sewage outlets	Population discharging from outlet	Type of treatment	Discharge point relative to LWM (Low Watter Mark)	Remarks	Track record
⌒⌒	Grouville 710501					Sandy. Occasionally affected by run off from land. A pleasant beach running parallel to a common and the Royal Grouville Golf Course.	✔✔

71. PLEMONT, JERSEY

OS ref: 561566

This is a relatively quiet beach, popular with the locals, in a compact sheltered bay situated in the north-west of the island. There is a steep climb down to the beach from the car park. This beach is ideal for the beach explorer as there are many fascinating caves.

Water quality

 Litter
There are bins in the car park.

 Bathing safety
Lifeguards in attendance from May to September.

Access
Access to the beach is via steep wooden slatted steps which would make access to the beach difficult for people with limited mobility.

P **Parking**
There is a car park serving this area at the top of the steps, however this can get very busy in the summer months.

Public transport
Bus number 8.

WC **Toilets**
There are public facilities near to the café before the final approach to the beach.

Food
There is a café at the top of the steps to the beach selling food and beach-type merchandise.

Wet weather alternatives
Due to the relatively unspoilt nature of the bay there are no indoor facilities apart from the café. However a short distance away are a couple of visitor attractions such as Plemont Candlecraft.

Wildlife and walks
A cliff path runs between

Plemont and Greve de l'Ecq. To the west the path goes to Les Landes which leads to a network of footpaths. This is a very exposed coastline and there are colonies of Puffins and Razorbills at Plemont.

Rating	Resort	Sewage outlets	Population discharging from outlet	Type of treatment	Discharge point relative to LWM (Low Watter Mark)	Remarks	Track record
⌒⌒	Greve de L' Ecq 582556					Sandy bay with rocky outcrops. Popular launch site for boats. The decrease in water quality at this site is being investigated and is thought to be agricultural run off.	✓✓

211

CHAPTER ELEVEN

BRITAIN'S COASTLINE UNDER THREAT

Sewage pollution is the reason why this book was written and sewage is a widespread problem. Around one thousand million litres (220 million gallons) of sewage are pumped into the sea around Britain every day. Most of this is either raw or simply screened. Sewage is a mixture of domestic waste water, cleaning agents, industrial and trade effluent, solid litter and storm water (run-off from road surfaces). Typically sewage will contain human wastes, engine oils from trade and domestic uses, fat balls from domestic and trade kitchens, and a range of heavy metal contaminants (mercury, lead, cadmium, arsenic, copper) from detergents, trade effluents and road surface run-off. It also contains viruses and bacteria that can cause disease in humans.

To catch a potentially fatal illness from sewage whilst bathing is rare, but Government studies show that there is a considerable chance of contracting other, minor illnesses. It is quite possible to contract an ear, nose and throat infection, or suffer diarrhoea and vomiting after swimming. The Marine Conservation Society receives many reports each year from people who have suffered quite serious illness after windsurfing or diving in sewage-contaminated waters.

When you consider what sewage is, what it can do and how much is produced in Britain, comprehensive treatment would seem an essential step to protect our health and the marine environment. However, very little sewage receives a proper standard of treatment in this country. Around 80% of major coastal out-falls (those serving over 10,000 people) discharge raw or screened sewage (screened sewage is effectively raw). Treating sewage properly is not difficult; a comprehensive sewage treatment system is described in the following pages.

The first stage is to try and remove all the larger solids, such as plastics, nappies and all manner of debris that finds its way into the sewers. This is done by screening the sewage, a very coarse filtering process, which is called PRELIMINARY TREATMENT. The material screened out is largely unrecyclable and will probably be disposed of in landfill sites or possibly incinerated. Preliminary treatment may also include a process called MACERATION, which is roughly equivalent to putting the sewage through a food blender.

The sewage at this stage will have suspended solids at between 200-500 milligrams per litre, so the next stage in a comprehensive treatment system is to allow the solids to settle out. This is known as PRIMARY TREATMENT. A standard sewage treatment works will allow for several hours of settlement before the effluent (the liquid remaining once the solids have precipitated) is passed on to the next stage. Primary treatment will remove 50-60% of suspended solids, and between 0-50% of bacteria and viruses. A large volume of sludge is produced by primary treatment.

The effluent from primary treatment is then subject to SECONDARY TREATMENT. This is biological treatment designed to reduce the oxygen demand of the sewage (the amount of oxygen that the effluent will need to be broken down completely in the sea). Secondary treatment may be achieved by a number of processes all of which generate more sludge which has to be dealt with. Secondary treatment can remove 90-95% of suspended solids, 80-90% of the oxygen demand, 75-99% of bacteria and viruses and about 50% of heavy metal contamination.

In some cases, though in the UK this is still rare, TERTIARY TREATMENT may be used to reduce the nitrogen and phosphorus levels in the effluent in order to lessen its fertiliser

Figure showing full sewage treatment.

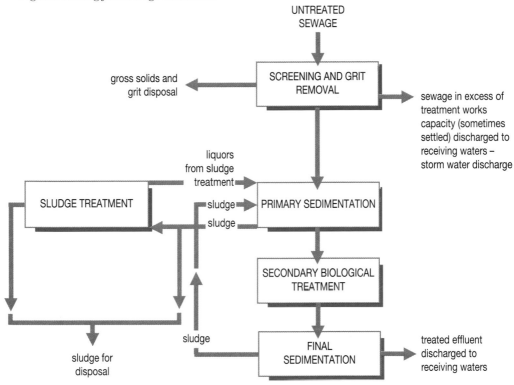

effect. This process is known as nutrient stripping.and is important since nutrients in sewage, like nitrogen and phosphorus, can severely disrupt marine ecosystems, causing algal blooms and the death of marine life. Some algal blooms which cause various forms of shellfish poisoning are enhanced by nutrient pollution.

Sewage is discharged to sea via OUT-FALL PIPES. These pipes vary in length. Many discharge a matter of a few metres below low water mark; some may even discharge above the level of low tide. In the past, the LONG SEA OUT-FALL was seen as the solution to contaminated bathing waters, but it is now regarded as no substitute for treating sewage. There are significant ecological problems with raw sewage wherever it is discharged. Sewage slicks from long sea out-falls may be washed back towards beaches by wind, waves and currents, and result in unpleasant encounters for swimmers and sailors

The SLUDGE generated by sewage treatment can be used in a variety of ways. Sewage sludge should not be regarded as a waste to be disposed of as quickly and cheaply as possible, but as a resource to be exploited. There are many options and sludge can be used for the production of fertilisers, soil conditioners, peat substitutes, methane production for electricity generation and even oil production. An innovative scheme piloted in Britain by Wessex Water, the Swiss Combi process, has shown that a commercial fertiliser can be made from sewage sludge.

At whatever stage the effluent is discharged to sea, whether raw or treated, CHEMICAL DISINFECTION may be applied. The chemicals used may include sodium hypochlorite, peracetic acid or ozone. None of these treatments has been adequately tested to ensure safety with regard to marine life and human health. There is also doubt about the efficacy of these methods in destroying the disease-causing agents in the effluent, so, the use of chemical disinfection may be lulling us into a false sense of security by removing the indicators of sewage pollution but not the source of pollution itself. It is widely agreed that chemical disinfection is no substitute for comprehensive sewage treatment. PHYSICAL DISINFECTION using ultrafiltration methods or possibly ultraviolet light treatment appears to present no threat to the marine environment, since these treatments are non-additive. The Marine Conservation Society actively supports physical disinfection systems as part of a comprehensive sewage treatment programme, to protect both public health and the marine environment.

Added to the routinely discharging out-falls are overflow out-falls. During storms and times of heavy rainfall, raw sewage is released from works that normally discharge treated sewage. On average storm water and overflow out-falls are used around 10 times a year as treatment works become overloaded and sewers fill up. Storm water outflows discharge completely untreated sewage – sometimes directly onto the beach above low water mark.

There is no doubt that improvements are being made to sewage treatment systems, but progress is slow. The water service companies have control over the vast majority of discharges and are directly responsible for cleaning up this large-scale pollution of our seas. Many of the companies appear to be doing only the absolute minimum required of them by law. There are three main pieces of legislation that refer directly to the discharge of sewage to the sea:

Under the Water Resources Act (1991) the National Rivers Authority (NRA) must have given consent to the water companies before any discharge to sea. These consents should be designed to protect the waters into which the sewage is being discharged. The NRA should put a limit on the amount of sewage that can be discharged to sea, but in practice the system does not always work effectively to reduce the impact of sewage and can be undermined by political considerations. Some coastal discharges regularly breach their consents and many simply do not have numerical consents, meaning that no limit is put on the volume of raw sewage that goes down the out-fall pipe and straight into the sea.

Unfortunately it is not just sewage that ends up in the sewers. A major problem still remaining is the ease with which industrial discharges to sewers may be made without the need for a direct licence from the NRA. This is a loophole which should be plugged at once. Industrial discharges can introduce all sorts of chemical pollutants, including heavy metals, industrial detergents, dyes and oils into the domestic sewers.

A European Community law, the Urban Waste Water Treatment Directive (91/27/EEC), seeks to make secondary treatment the standard level of treatment for all coastal sewage discharges which serve populations of more than 10,000 people and estuarine discharges which serve more than 2,000 people. Full implementation of the Directive will undoubtedly see an improvement in the coastal waters around Britain. The Directive itself is not entirely satisfactory, since numerous smaller out-falls are not covered, and primary treatment will be considered adequate for large out-falls if the coastal waters are declared less sensitive. More worrying than this is the current attitude of the Government; this Government signed the Directive with complete knowledge of its implications in 1991, but, they are now calling for a slow-down in its implementation due to cost. They are also asking the other member states of the European Commission to reconsider their position on the Directive. Britain appears to be as enthusiastic for the Urban Waste Water Treatment Directive as it was for the Bathing Water Directive when the Government identified only 27 bathing waters in Britain; land-locked Luxembourg declared 34. The Urban Waste Water Treatment Directive must be implemented. In asking for a delay and increased phasing in the implementation of the Directive, the Government is asking us to live with sewage pollution and a degraded and degrading coastline for even longer.

The Government is now considering the ratification of Annex IV of the International Agreement on the Prevention of Pollution from Ships (MARPOL). Annex IV of MARPOL makes it an offence in many cases to discharge, without treatment, sewage from ships and large boats and yachts. Holding tanks on ships are to be encouraged so that sewage can be discharged to land-based sewage treatment works at ports and harbours. Reception facilities at ports must be adequate to cope. However, there is no point in bringing raw sewage back to land, if the land-based treatment is simply to discharge it back to sea via an out-fall pipe. While this agreement is a step in the right direction, there are many countries with large shipping fleets operating around the coastline that do not recognise the MARPOL Agreement and will still discharge raw sewage. Boat owners wanting guidance on how to deal with sewage should contact the Royal Yachting Association and ask for a copy of their code of conduct – the Clean Code for Boat Owners and Users.

Despite the many treatment methods available, and the legal framework designed to protect the seas, the simple fact is that much of the sewage from coastal populations is discharged raw or simply screened. While that is the case, those using beaches and bathing waters will still suffer from illnesses caught in the water and be disgusted by the sewage-related debris on the beach. We can all help with the sewage debris problem, by simply not flushing sanitary items, condoms or cotton buds, but by binning them instead. This will help clean up beaches and bathing waters, as well as making the water companies' treatment of sewage easier. The machinery would be subject to fewer breakdowns and pipes to fewer blockages if there was less debris in the sewers.

It is not only sewage-related debris that is apparent on the beaches; other debris appears despite the fact that it shouldn't be there. The Environmental Protection Act 1990 made it illegal to drop or otherwise deposit litter in public places on land, including beaches. Much of the litter found on beaches has been washed up by the sea. To drop litter at sea is also illegal under Annex V of MARPOL, which prohibits the dumping of plastics overboard from ships and boats. In British waters this aspect of MARPOL is regulated under the Merchant Shipping (Prevention of Pollution by Garbage) Regulations 1988 which appears to be inadequately enforced with only one prosecution to date. Furthermore, compliance with Annex V is voluntary, and it has been ratified by only 65% of gross shipping tonnage of the world fleet. Many ships undoubtedly still dump plastics over the side whilst at sea, adding to the debris on the beaches.

We all have a responsibility. When you go to the seaside, just as in the countryside or in the city centre, you should put all your rubbish in the bin or take it home with you. Remember that it is an offence to drop litter anywhere in public. Litter is unsightly and dangerous. Drink cans and glass bottles are particularly dangerous – there is no excuse at all for leaving these lying around, especially since they can be taken for recycling in most towns.

Coastlines are also affected by accidents, such as the horrific oil spills in the Gulf, the *Exxon Valdez* incident in Alaska in 1989 and the *Braer* in 1993. With such incidents happening most years you could be forgiven for thinking that these major disasters were the main source of oil pollution of the seas. In fact these sorts of accidents account for only around 10% of the oil that finds its way into the sea each year. It is difficult to believe that the bulk of oil pollution comes from routine losses and controllable discharges. Continual chronic oil pollution is caused by the deliberate and illegal flushing of tanks at sea by the bulk oil carriers, spills at on-shore and offshore oil installations during the loading and unloading of tankers, and pipeline fractures which can allow tonnes of oil to escape into the seas each year. The most visible sign of oil pollution on beaches is the

THE MARINE CONSERVATION SOCIETY
9 Gloucester Road,
Ross-on-Wye,
Herefordshire,
HR9 5BU.
Telephone: 0989-66017
Fax: 0989-67815

THE COASTGUARD
The Coastguard is available to help anyone in danger at sea or on the beach. If you think that someone needs help at sea, DON'T HESITATE – dial 999 and ask for the Coastguard – DON'T LEAVE IT TO SOMEONE ELSE!

The Coastguard must also be told immediately of any dangerous items washed up on the beach, such as chemical drums and old wartime explosives. If you're in doubt, call anyway. The call is always free.

The National Rivers Authority (NRA) – England and Wales

NRA Pollution Hotline:
0800-807060

NRA Head Office,
Rivers House,
Waterside Drive,
Aztec West,
Almondsbury,
Bristol.
BS12 4UD.
Telephone: 0454-624400
Fax: 0454-624409

London Office,
Eastbury House,
30-34, Albert Embankment,
London.
SE1 7TL.
Telephone: 071-820-0101
Fax: 071-820-1603

NRA Anglican Region,
Kingfisher House,
Goldhay Way,
Orton Goldhay,
Peterborough.
PE2 0ZR.
Telephone: 0733-371811
Fax: 0733-231840

NRA Northumbria and Yorkshire Region,
21, Park Square South,
Leeds.
LS1 2QG.
Telephone: 0532-440191
Fax: 0532-461889

Gosforth Office,
Eldon House,
Regent Centre,
Gosforth,
Newcastle upon Tyne.
NE3 3UD.
Telephone: 091-213-0266
Fax: 091-284-5069

NRA North West Region,
PO Box 12,
Richard Fairclough House,
Knutsford Road,
Warrington.
WA14 1HG.
Telephone: 0925-53999
Fax: 0925-415961

NRA Severn Trent Region,
Sapphire East,
550, Streetsbrook Road,
Solihull,
West Midlands.
B91 1QT.
Telephone: 021-711-2324
Fax: 021-711-5824

NRA Southern Region,
Guildbourne House,
Chatsworth Road,
Worthing
Surrey.
BN11 1LD.
Telephone: 0903-820692
Fax: 0903-821832

NRA Southwestern Region,
Manley House,
Kestrel Way,
Exeter.
Devon.
EX2 7LQ.
Telephone: 0392-444000
Fax: 0392-444238

Bridgwater Office,
Rivers House,
East Quay,
Bridgwater,
Somerset.
TA6 4YS.
Telephone: 0278-457333
Fax: 0278-452985

NRA Thames Region,
Kings Meadow House,
Kings Meadow Road,
Reading.
RG1 8DQ.
Telephone: 0734-535000
Fax: 0734-500388

NRA Welsh Region,
Rivers House,
St Mellons Business Park,
St Mellons,
Cardiff.
CF3 0FT.
Telephone: 0222-770088
Fax: 0222-798555

THE RIVER PURIFICATION BOARDS – SCOTLAND

Highlands RPB,
Carr's Corner,
Lochybridge,
Fort William,
Inverness-shire.
PH33 6TQ.
0397-704351

North East RPB,
Greyhope House,
Greyhope Road,
Torry,
Aberdeen.
AB1 3RD.
0224-248338

Forth RPB,
Heriot Watt Research Park,
Avenue North,
Riccarton,
Edinburgh.
031-449-7296

Clyde RPB,
Rivers House,
Murray Road,
East Kilbride,
Glasgow.
G75 0LA.
03552-38181

Tweed RPB,
Burnbrae,
Mossilee Road,
Galashiels.
TD1 1NF.
0896-2425

Solway RPB,
Rivers House,
Irongray Road,
Dumfries.
DG2 0JE.
0387-720502

Tay RPB,
1 South Street,
Perth.
PH2 8NJ.
0738-27989

DEPARTMENT OF THE ENVIRONMENT FOR NORTHERN IRELAND (DOE – NI)

Environmental Protection Division,
Calvert House,
23 Castle Place,
Belfast.
BT1 1FY.
0232-230560

THE WATER SERVICE COMPANIES (WSC'S), England and Wales

South West Water,
Peninsula House,
Rydon Lane,
Exeter.
EX2 7HR.
0392-219666

Wessex Water,
Wessex House,
Passage Street,
Bristol.
BS2 0JQ.
0272-290611

Southern Water,
Southern House,
Yeoman Road,
Worthing.
BN13 3NX.
0903-64444

Thames Water,
Nugent House,
Vastern Road,
Reading.
RG1 8DB.
0734-591159

Anglian Water,
Ambury Road,
Huntingdon.
PE18 6NZ.
0480-433433

Yorkshire Water,
Broadacre House,
Vicar Lane,
Bradford
BD1 5PZ.
0274-306063

Northumbrian Water,
Abbey Road,
Pity Me,
Durham.
DH1 5FJ.
091-384-4222

North West Water,
Dawson House,
Great Sankey,
Warrington.
WA5 3LW.
0925-234000

Severn-Trent Water,
2297 Coventry Road,
Sheldon,
Birmingham.
B26 3PU.
021-722-4000

Welsh Water,
Plas-y-Ffynnon,
Cambrian Way,
Brecon,
Powys.
LD3 7HP.
0874-3181

THE SCOTTISH REGIONAL COUNCILS

Borders Regional Council,
Water and Sewerage Department,
Regional Headquarters,
Newtown St Boswells,
Melrose,
Roxburghshire,
TD6 0SA.
Tel: 0835-23301

Central Regional Council,
Water and Sewerage Department,
Viewforth,
Stirling.
FK8 2ET.
Tel: 0786-442000

Dumfries and Galloway Regional Council,
Water and Sewerage Department,
Regional Council Offices,
English Street,
Dumfries.
DG1 2DD.
Tel: 0387 61234

Fife Regional Council,
Water and Sewerage Department,
Regional Headquarters,
Fife House,
North Street,
Glenrothes,
Fife.
KY7 5LT.
Tel: 0592 754411

Grampian Regional Council,
Water and Sewerage Department,
Woodhill House,
Westburn Road,
Aberdeen.
AB9 2LU.
Tel: 0224 682222

Highland Regional Council, •
Water and Sewerage Department,
Regional Buildings,
Glenurquhart Road,
Inverness.
IV3 5NX.
Tel: 0463 702000

Lothian Regional Council,
Water and Sewerage Department,
Regional Headquarters,
George IV Bridge,
Edinburgh.
EH1 1UG.
Tel: 031 229 9292

Strathcylde Regional Council,
Water and Sewerage Department,
20, India Street,
Glasgow.
G2 4PF.
Tel: 041 204 2900

Tayside Regional Council,
Water and Sewerage Department,
Bullion House,
Invergowrie,
Dundee.
DD2 5BB.
Tel: 0382 23281

Orkney Island Authority,
Council Offices,
School Place,
Kirkwall,
Orkney.
KW15 1NY.
Tel: 0856 3535

Shetland Islands Authority,
Council Offices,
Town Hall,
Lerwick,
Shetland.
ZE1 0HB.
Tel: 0595 3535

Western Isles Authority,
Council Offices,
Sandwick Road,
Stornoway,
Isle of Lewis.
PA87 2BW.
Tel: 0851 703773

LEISURE AND RECREATION CONTACTS

The National Trust,
36, Queen Annes Gate,
London.
SW1H OAS.

The National Trust For Scotland,
5, Charlotte Square,Edinburgh,
EH2 4DU.

The Manx National Trust,
The Manx Museum,
Douglas,
Isle of Man.

The Isles of Scilly Environmental Trust,
Hamewith,
The Parade,
St Mary's,
Isles of Scilly.
TR21 0LP

The Heritage Coast Forum,
Manchester Polytechnic,
Bellhouse Building,
Lower Ormond Street,
Manchester.
M15 6BX

Central Council for British Naturism
Assurance House,
35-41 Hazelwood Road,
Northampton.
NN1 1LL.

The Royal Yachting Association
RYA House,
Romsey House,
Eastleigh,
Hampshire.
S05 4YA.

British Sub Aqua Club,
Telford's Quay,
Ellesmere Port,
South Wirral,
Cheshire.
L65 4FY.

INDEX

1:50 000 Landranger Series Map
CONVENTIONAL SIGNS

Ordnance Survey

ROADS AND PATHS   Not necessarily rights of way

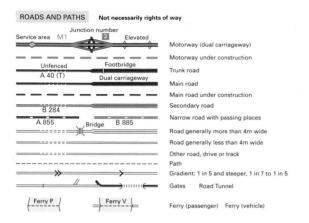

Junction number M1 Service area ... Elevated	Motorway (dual carriageway)
	Motorway under construction
Unfenced Footbridge A 40 (T) Dual carriageway	Trunk road
	Main road
	Main road under construction
B 284	Secondary road
A 855 Bridge B 885	Narrow road with passing places
	Road generally more than 4m wide
	Road generally less than 4m wide
	Other road, drive or track
	Path
	Gradient: 1 in 5 and steeper, 1 in 7 to 1 in 5
	Gates Road Tunnel
Ferry P Ferry V	Ferry (passenger) Ferry (vehicle)

RAILWAYS

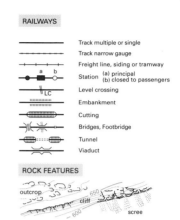

	Track multiple or single
	Track narrow gauge
	Freight line, siding or tramway
a b	Station (a) principal (b) closed to passengers
LC	Level crossing
	Embankment
	Cutting
	Bridges, Footbridge
	Tunnel
	Viaduct

ROCK FEATURES

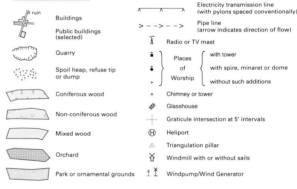

outcrop   cliff   scree

PUBLIC RIGHTS OF WAY   (Not applicable to Scotland)

··················	Footpath
─ ─ ─ ─ ─	Bridleway
─·─·─·─·─	Road used as public path
-+-+-+-+-+	Byway open to all traffic

Public rights of way indicated by these symbols have been derived from Definitive Maps as amended by later enactments or instruments held by Ordnance Survey on   (date)   and are shown subject to the limitations imposed by the scale of mapping. Later information may be obtained from the appropriate County or London Borough Council

The representation on this map of any other road, track or path is no evidence of a right of way

Danger Area   Firing and Test Ranges in the area. Danger! Observe warning notices

HEIGHTS

50	Contours are at 10 metres vertical interval
144	Heights are to the nearest metre above mean sea level

Heights shown close to a triangulation pillar refer to the station height at ground level and not necessarily to the summit.

1 metre = 3.2808 feet

WATER FEATURES

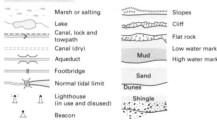

	Marsh or salting		Slopes
	Lake		Cliff
	Canal, lock and towpath		Flat rock
	Canal (dry)		Low water mark
	Aqueduct	Mud	High water mark
	Footbridge		
	Normal tidal limit	Sand	
	Lighthouse (in use and disused)	Dunes	
	Beacon	Shingle	

GENERAL FEATURES

ruin	Buildings		Electricity transmission line (with pylons spaced conventionally)
	Public buildings (selected)	> --> -->	Pipe line (arrow indicates direction of flow)
	Quarry		Radio or TV mast
	Spoil heap, refuse tip or dump		Places of Worship with tower / with spire, minaret or dome / without such additions
	Coniferous wood	○	Chimney or tower
	Non-coniferous wood		Glasshouse
	Mixed wood	+	Graticule intersection at 5' intervals
	Orchard	Ⓗ	Heliport
	Park or ornamental grounds	△	Triangulation pillar
			Windmill with or without sails
			Windpump/Wind Generator

ABBREVIATIONS

P	Post office
PH	Public house
MS	Milestone
MP	Milepost
CH	Clubhouse
PC	Public convenience (in rural areas)
TH	Town Hall, Guildhall or equivalent
CG	Coastguard

ANTIQUITIES

VILLA	Roman
Castle	Non-Roman
✕1066	Battlefield (with date)
∴	Tumulus
+	Position of antiquity which cannot be drawn to scale
𝕸	Ancient Monuments and Historic Buildings in the care of the Secretaries of State for the Environment, for Scotland and for Wales and that are open to the public

The revision date of archaeological information varies over the sheet

BOUNDARIES

+ — + — +	National
-•- •- •-	London Borough
-+- +- +-	District
─•─••─•─	County, Region or Islands Area
	National Park or Forest Park

NT National Trust   NT always open
                        NT limited access, observe local signs

NTS (in red or blue) National Trust for Scotland

TOURIST INFORMATION

	Information centre, all year/seasonal	⨯	Picnic site	▲	Youth hostel
	Selected places of tourist interest	Å	Camp site	⌐	Golf course or links
	Viewpoint		Caravan site		Bus or coach station
P	Parking				Public telephone
					Motoring organisation telephone
				PC	Public convenience (in rural areas)